P9-DUJ-243

THE IVY

Gulls Eggs (2) with Celery Salt   7.75

HORS D'OEUVRES

Mixed Eastern Hors d'Oeuvres 7.75	Bang Bang Chicken 5.75	Plum Tomato & Basil Galette 6.25	Steak Tartare 7.50/14.75
Baked Leek & Trompette Tart with Truffle Oil 7.50	Hoummus with Chickpea Relish 6.25 *served with Lebanese flat bread*	Sautéed Foie Gras 13.75 *with onion galette and sauternes jus*	Sevruga Caviar 30g/50g 28.50/48.50 *with blinis and sour cream*

SALADS

Caesar Salad *made with romaine and iceberg lettuce*	5.75	Pousse Spinach and Roquefort Salad	7.00	Truffled Mixed Artichokes *with corn salad and herbs*	9.75
Crispy Duck and Watercress Salad	7.50	Rocket and Parmesan Salad	6.00	Mixed Tomatoes and Basil Salad	4.50
Belgian Endive Salad *with pommery mustard dressing*	4.25	Griddled Chicken Salad *with piquillos and guacamole*	11.25	Salad of Fried Egg, Lardons and Landcress	5.75

SOUPS

Spring Vegetable & Bean Broth	4.75	Spiced Chicken & Coconut Soup	5.75	Creamed Wild Mushroom Soup	5.25

SEAFOOD

Potted Shrimps *with landcress and wholemeal toast*	9.75	Hot & Sour Wonton Prawns 9.50		Dressed Cornish Crab *with celeriac remoulade*	12.50	Roasted Scallops *with crispy bacon and baby sorrel* 12.75

EGGS AND PASTA

Smoked Salmon with Scrambled Eggs 7.75/11.75	Spaghetti ai Funghi 7.50/11.50	Fettucine with Lobster 13.75/19.75 and Tarragon	Corned Beef Hash with Fried Egg 7.75
Risotto Nero 8.75/11.75	Eggs Benedict 5.00/10.50	Risotto of Butternut Squash and Parmesan 7.50/9.50	Spiced Pumpkin Tortelloni 7.50/9.50

FISH

Char-Grilled Fish of the Day 14.75 *served garnished*	Salmon Fishcake 9.75 *with sorrel sauce and sautéed spinach*	Herb Baked Cod 13.25 *with buttered leaf greens and a red wine sauce*	Seared Yellow Fin Tuna 14.50 *with a plum tomato and green herb relish*
Deep Fried Lemon Sole, with Minted Pea Puree, Chips and Tartare Sauce 11.75	Roast Fillet of Seabass 19.75 *with samphire and spiced lentils*	Kedgeree 8.75 *made with smoked haddock, salmon and wild mushrooms*	Char-Grilled Red Mullet and Squid 15.75 *with olive mash and tapenade*

ROASTS AND GRILLS

The Ivy Hamburger 8.50 *7oz. fully garnished*	Breast of Corn Fed Chicken 10.50 *with szechuan vegetables and soy*	Pork & Leek Sausages 9.50 *with creamed leek mash and mustard sauce*	Char-Grilled Rib Eye Steak 15.25 *with sauce béarnaise*
Calf's Liver and Bacon 15.75 *with sage, onions and mash*	Grilled Rabbit with Rosemary 15.75 *on creamed polenta and black olives*	Roast Poulet des Landes 30.00 *with truffle jus and dauphin potato (for 2 persons)*	Rosemary-Skewered Lambs' Kidneys 9.75 *with a barolo risotto*

ENTREES

Shepherds Pie 9.25 *made with lamb & beef*	Cassoulet de Toulouse au Confit de Canard 14.75	Escalope of Veal Holstein 15.50 *with anchovies, capers and fried egg*	Curried Chicken Masala 9.25 *with cardamom rice*

VEGETABLES AND POTATOES

				Bubble & Squeak	2.50
Sprouting Broccoli with Hollandaise	3.75	Parmesan Fried Courgettes with Pesto	4.00	Gratin of Butternut Squash 3.75	Buttery Mash 2.25
Mixed Spring Greens	2.75	Honey Roasted Parsnips	2.50	Truffled Green Beans 3.75	Pommes Allumettes 3.00
				Leaf Spinach 4.75	Medium Cut Chips 3.00

DESSERTS, PUDDINGS AND SAVOURIES

Welsh Rarebit 4.00	Sticky Toffee Pudding 5.75	Cinnamon Roasted Fruits with Mascarpone 6.25	Rippled Chocolate Ice Cream 5.50 with Bitter Chocolate Sauce
Herring Roes on Toast 4.50	Mousse aux deux Chocolats 5.50	Scandinavian Iced Berries with White Chocolate Sauce 6.25	Baked Alaska 11.50 *(for 2 persons)*
Farmhouse Cheddar with Crumpets and Onion Chutney 6.00	Cappuccino Brûlé 6.00		
	Baked Mascarpone Custard with Rhubarb 5.50	Tarte aux Pommes Chantilly 5.75	Bramley Apple Crumble 5.25 with Devonshire Clotted Cream

COFFEES AND TEAS

Coffee: Ethiopian, Full Roast:				Selection Fauchon:		2.00
Espresso	2.00	Filter	2.25	Darjeeling	Camomile	Earl Grey
	large 2.50	Cappuccino	2.75	Mint	Verveine	Jasmine
Ivy Chocolate Truffles (2)	2.00	Fresh Ground Decaffeinated Coffee Available				

THE IVY

The Restaurant and its Recipes

AA GILL

Hodder & Stoughton

Copyright © 1997 A A Gill, Christopher Corbin and Jeremy King
First published in 1997 by Hodder and Stoughton. A division of Hodder Headline PLC

The right of A A Gill, Christopher Corbin and Jeremy King to be identified as the Authors of the Work
has been asserted by them in accordance with the Copyright, Designs and Patents Act 1988.

All rights reserved. No part of this publication may be reproduced, stored in a retrieval system, or
transmitted, in any form or by any means without the prior written permission of the publisher, nor
be otherwise circulated in any form of binding or cover other than that in which it is published and
without a similar condition being imposed on the subsequent purchaser.

British Library Cataloguing in Publication Data
ISBN: 0 340 69312 6

Printed and bound in Italy

B/W Photography: Harriet Logan and pages 90–91
Colour Photography: Henry Bourne
Photography pages 62–3: Hugo Glendinning
Endpapers: *The Ivy Menu*, Tom Phillips (1990)
Design and Art Direction: Suzi Godson, Design 4

Hodder and Stoughton
A division of Hodder Headline PLC
338 Euston Road
London NW1 3BH

THE HISTORY

Nobody is certain exactly when the Ivy opened but around 1917 Abel Giandellini purchased what was a modest café that quickly gained favour with the theatre community. The name itself originated from a chance remark by the actress Alice Delysia, who overheard Monsieur Abel apologise to a customer for the inconvenience caused by building works. When he said that it was because of his intention to create a restaurant of the highest class, she interjected 'Don't worry – we will always come and see you. "We will cling together like the ivy,"' a line from a popular song.

Mario Gallati later joined M. Abel, and was instrumental in transforming the Ivy; the subsequent redevelopment of the premises produced a dining room which largely resembles the restaurant as it is today.

In 1945 Mario Gallati left to open Le Caprice. Between his departure and the acquisition of the restaurant by Chris Corbin and Jeremy King in 1989, the Ivy passed through several hands. Sold by M. Abel to Bernard Walsh of Wheelers in 1950, it was later owned by Joseph Melatini, Lady Grade and the Forte organisation.

The Ivy was relaunched in 1990: the architect M J Long carried out the refurbishment, with leading contemporary artists commissioned to create site-specific works. Restored to its former glory, it now seems firmly re-established as London's favourite theatre restaurant.

THE IVY ARTISTS

David Bailey	Barry Flanagan	Bill Jacklin	Sir Eduardo Paolozzi
Clive Barker	Future Systems	Allen Jones	Tom Phillips
Peter Blake	David Gryn	Michael Craig-Martin	Liz Rideal
Patrick Caulfield	Sir Howard Hodgkin	Janet Nathan	Joe Tilson

Weights, Measures and Servings

All recipes serve eight unless otherwise stated and are written to metric.
They can be converted successfully to imperial by using the following tables except the pastry recipes where only metric should be used. Do not combine metric and imperial.

Standards Liquid

1 tsp	=	5 ml
1 tbsp	=	15 ml
1 fl oz	=	30 ml
1 ml	=	0.35 ml
1 pint	=	20 fl oz
1 litre	=	35 fl oz

Standards Solid

1 oz	=	30 g
1 lb	=	16 oz (480 g)
1 g	=	0.35 oz
1 kg	=	2.2 lb

Liquid Conversions

Metric	Imperial
15 ml	$\frac{1}{2}$ fl oz
20 ml	$\frac{2}{3}$ fl oz
30 ml	1 fl oz
50 ml	1 $\frac{2}{3}$ fl oz
60 ml	2 fl oz
90 ml	3 fl oz
100 ml	3$\frac{1}{3}$ fl oz
150 ml	5 fl oz ($\frac{1}{4}$ pint)
200 ml	6$\frac{2}{3}$ fl oz
250 ml	8 fl oz
300 ml	10 fl oz ($\frac{1}{2}$ pint)
500 ml	16$\frac{2}{3}$ fl oz
600 ml	20 fl oz (1 pint)
1 litre	1$\frac{3}{4}$ pints
4 litres	7 pints

Solid Weight Conversions

Metric	Imperial
5g	$\frac{1}{6}$ oz
10g	$\frac{1}{3}$ oz
15 g	$\frac{1}{2}$ oz
30 g	1 oz
50g	1 $\frac{2}{3}$ oz
60 g	2 oz
90 g	3 oz
100 g	3 $\frac{1}{3}$ oz
150 g	5 oz
200 g	6 $\frac{2}{3}$ oz
250 g	8 $\frac{1}{3}$ oz
300 g	10 oz
400 g	13 $\frac{1}{2}$ oz
480 g	16 oz (1lb)
500 g	16 $\frac{2}{3}$ oz

Oven Temperature Conversions

°C	Gas	°F
110	$\frac{1}{4}$	225
120	$\frac{1}{2}$	250
140	1	275
150	2	300
160	3	325
175	4	350
190	5	375
200	6	400
220	7	425
230	8	450
240	9	475
260	10	500

Contents

The Recipes

ACKNOWLEDGEMENTS

All books are to some extent collaborations; this one was more than most. Resisting the urge to refer to everyone as ingredients in a bouillabaisse or course in a banquet, let me say an ungarnished but heartfelt thank you to Mark Hix, Executive Chef, for writing the recipes; to Des McDonald, Head Chef; Mitchell Everard, General Manager, and their respective brigades for all their help, courtesy and enthusiasm. To the invaluable Caroline McAuley, who turns my barely legible musing into pristine copy, and finally to Nicola Formby, who did all the research and liaison for this book, cooked sensational lunches and dinners whilst testing the recipes, and angelically did all the washing-up.

THE IVY

6.45 A.M. THE IVY. The day begins. The head plongeur - the chief washer, wiper, mopper, shifter, lifter, stacker, peeler, plucker and muttering-swearer - unlocks the heavy green double doors of the tradesmen's entrance and goes down the stairs, two at a time, past the service bar, the wine cellar, the condiments cupboard, the chef's glass-walled office, to the kitchen.

Outside it's chilly, down here it's warm. The conserved heat of thousands of dinners. A successful kitchen never knows what it is to be cold. Neon flickers and chunters over the room. Everything rests at attention. This kitchen looks like the engine room of a beached battleship, all iron and steel pipes and ducts, thick and corrugated, worn rough and smooth by use. It is a room that shrugs off the word 'design', like oil on a hot pan. It defies order or elegance. The equipment squats like sideboard sumos, nutted and bolted, defending their small territories.

A commercial kitchen is as different from a domestic one as a tiger is from a tabby. There are none of the small rustic niceties of a family home and hearth here. This is not a warm welcome by the stove, no smiley magnets on the fridge, no children's daubs pinned to the wall, hanging herbs, aesthetic vases of wooden spoons. There is not a single chair - no time for one. This is a war room, a factory that manufactures hand-made food with dozens of moving parts, dozens of temperatures, textures, liquid, solid, ice, fire, propelled with pinpoint accuracy and machine-gun rapidity, plate after plate, the same and unique.

The plongeur doesn't look at the kitchen. He could trace every shin-barking stanchion, every apron-snagging tap in his sleep. He gets his brushes, buckets, cloths and sticky acid to attack the canopy. Every morning starts with the canopy. The long steel chimney that stretches over the central island of the ovens, the hot heart of the kitchen. The canopy is a bugger. It sucks the fumes, smoke and hot oaths of service in one continuous day-long intake of breath and spews, exhales, up, up, up and out, into the exhausted sky, to mix with all those other heavenly burnt offerings of London at the trough. The canopy is a bugger. Oil, fat, dripping, lard, ghee, stick and congeal in its creases and seams. The steam-borne smells of root and muscle, allium and brassica, saffron, thyme, turmeric, allspice, nutmeg and cinnamon, caramelised sugar, brandy and sour vinegar, duck thighs and salmon scales curl and emulsify into gobbets that dribble into nubbed stalactites on its galvanised yawn. In other restaurants they try to forget about the canopy, pretend it's not there. Ignore its acquisitory intake of breath, leave it to someone else. Once a week, once a month, whenever the Health Inspector cometh. The Ivy is not other restaurants. At the Ivy they do the bugger every damn day.

A commis-chef arrives, thin and pale as bacon rind, eyes rheumy with untouched sleep. Slope-shuffling feet, he goes to the hob, turns a key, strikes a match. The first hissing blue flame. A commis isn't quite the lowest being in the brigade of chefs: there are apprentices below him, but he is non-commissioned, expendable fodder. Commis is the beginning of the long climb to your own kitchen, your own glass office, but it's a long way away this morning. He bangs down a pan. In every kitchen in the world this is the first thing ever cooked: water. The start of everything, the universal necessity. You can get by without anything but water. Water for coffee. Big tin of instant. Instant, peel away the memories of warm sheets. Instant, wash-the-gritty-eyes caffeine. All the staff here drink from half-pint mugs. The customers have cups and saucers, but this isn't sipping and chatting coffee: this is medicine, this is drugs.

The commis swigs, then collects a heavy sticky blue dustbin on dodgy wheels, a mobile charnel house, full of claggy bones. Big, saw-ended, clubbable veal bones, baked brown and congealed. He puts a pot, big enough to boil a small missionary, on to the wide burner and chucks in skeleton segments two-handed. This cauldron, and another like it, will simmer and bubble all day, washing the knuckles and marrow of flavour, until the bones are bleached dry. This stock is the fuel of traditional kitchens, the basic sticky, meaty, chameleon goodness, that is the base for soups, sauces and glazes. The Ivy makes and uses up to fifty litres a day. Another swig of medicine. Trays of stacked fresh bones go into the slow oven to be browned off for tomorrow.

The kitchen begins to fill. The morning sous-chef arrives - he is in charge until lunch - and starts going through papers in the crammed glass office. Upstairs, beyond the swing doors that mark the uneasy boundary between the white uniform and the black, the restaurant is still dark and quiet. The tables and chairs are stacked in the middle of the room, silhouetted against the faint grey dawn that pokes through the criss-crossed mullioned windows. An empty restaurant is never a lonely place. The bubble and clatter of service seem to be just a sub-audible echo away. The room hums with the spirit of dinner.

At the far end, through the bar and the doors into the lobby where the hat-check sits, there is a blue window with a moon on it. A street light shines and casts a romantic, dream-like, cerulean glow over the entrance. It is appropriate. The Ivy is a romantic place.

The Ivy is a unique restaurant. In a city bowed down with restaurants, these fretted, scarred, screwed and glued plywood upended tables and chairs are the most sought after in Britain. More people yearn for a round plywood first-night table than a Georgian pedestal table with acanthus carving. In the trade the Ivy has a professional reputation that is envied beyond avarice and mimicked thanks. This is the pre-eminent club of the British theatre, drama's green room. It is also claimed for television, film, publishing, advertising and journalism. This is the room where people who are professionally good in rooms come to be good at what they are good at. The Ivy is a modern, living Poets' Corner. At every lunch or dinner, anyone who reads a Sunday paper will recognise at least a dozen relaxed, smooth-toothed, autocue animated faces, and the ones you don't recognise are likely to be the movers and shakers, the fixers and dealers of the culture.

Other restaurants may drop a handful of starry names of who eats with them. At the Ivy it would be easier to list the ones who don't. Noël Coward doesn't eat here, Laurence Olivier, Margot Fonteyn, Marlene Dietrich and Dame Nellie Melba don't eat here, but they did. For most of this century everybody who is anybody has dined at the Ivy. ➢33

Stocks and Soups

Stocks

A hundred kilos of veal, chicken and fish bones arrive daily in the kitchen at the Ivy to make stocks for sauces and soups.

At home it is useful to keep some concentrated stocks in the freezer: if you need a litre, it's just as quick to make five and concentrate what you don't use. Freeze it in little tubs; when you need it, defrost it and add water. Here are four simple stocks that you will need for recipes throughout the book. The quantities given for each provide 5 litres. If you plan to order the bones in advance from your butcher ask him to chop them into pieces as you will get more bones in your pot and more flavour in your stock.

Dark Meat Stock

2 kg beef, veal, lamb or chicken bones, chopped
3 medium onions, peeled and chopped
5 medium carrots, peeled and chopped
1 small head celery, chopped
2 leeks, trimmed, washed and chopped
$1/2$ bulb of garlic, roughly chopped
50 g tomato purée
20 black peppercorns
10 g thyme
1 bay leaf

Pre-heat the oven to 200°C /gas mark 6. Wash the bones in cold water to remove any blood. Then roast them with the vegetables for about 15-20 minutes until they are lightly coloured, giving them a good turn every so often.

When everything is a nice golden brown colour, add the tomato purée and stir well. Return the pan to the oven for another 10 minutes. Put the bones and vegetables into a large pot, cover them with water and add the rest of the ingredients. Bring it to the boil, skim off any scum that forms and simmer for 3-4 hours. During cooking the stock will need topping up with water to keep the ingredients covered, and skimming occasionally.

Strain through a fine-meshed sieve and remove any fat with a ladle. Check its strength and reduce it if necessary.

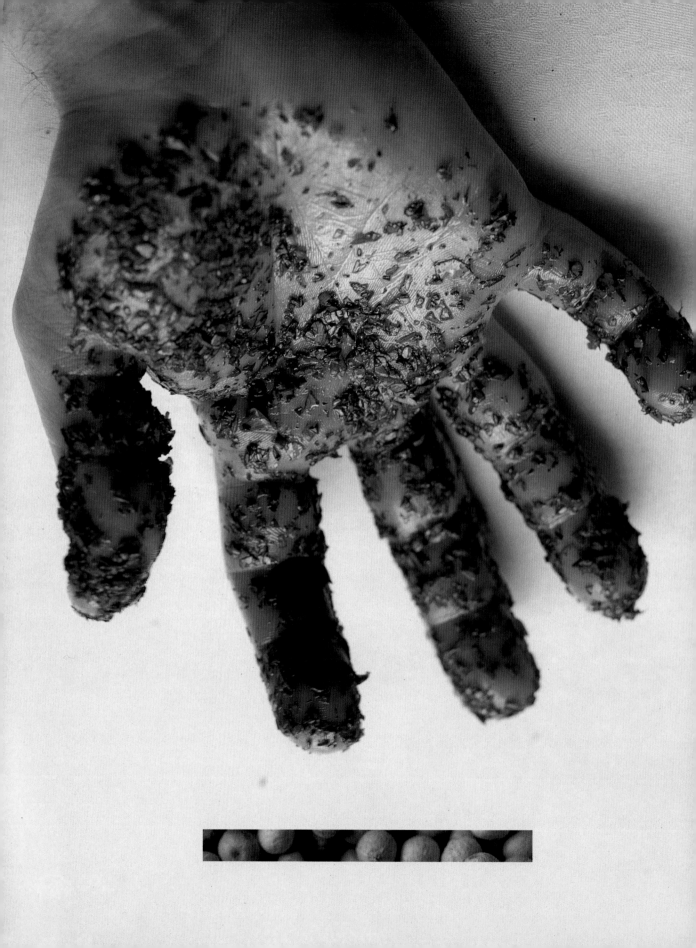

Chicken Stock

2 kg chicken bones, chopped
3 medium leeks, trimmed, washed and chopped
3 medium onions, peeled and chopped
1 small head celery, chopped

10 g thyme
1 bay leaf
20 black peppercorns

Wash the chicken bones to remove any blood. Put them into a pot with the rest of the ingredients and cover everything with cold water. Bring to the boil, skim off any scum that forms and simmer for 2 hours. During cooking, the stock may need topping up with water to keep the ingredients covered, and skimming occasionally. Strain through a fine-meshed sieve and remove any fat with a ladle. Check its strength and reduce if necessary.

Fish Stock

2 kg white fish bones, sole, turbot, brill, etc.
2 medium leeks, trimmed, washed and chopped
2 medium onions, peeled and chopped
1/2 head celery, chopped
1/2 lemon

1 tsp fennel seeds
20 black peppercorns
5 g thyme
1 bay leaf
a handful of parsley

Wash the bones in cold water. Put them into a pot with the rest of the ingredients, cover with cold water and bring it to the boil. Skim off any scum that forms and simmer for 20 minutes, skimming occasionally. Strain through a fine-meshed sieve. Check its strength and reduce if necessary.

Vegetable Stock

3 medium onions, peeled and chopped
1 small head celery, chopped
3 leeks, trimmed, washed and chopped
5 medium carrots, peeled and chopped

2 bay leaves
5 g thyme
20 black peppercorns
a handful of parsley
1 tsp fennel seeds

Put all the ingredients into a pot and cover with cold water. Bring it to the boil, skim off any scum that forms and simmer for 30–40 minutes. Strain through a fine-meshed sieve. Check its strength and reduce if necessary.

Iced Plum Tomato Soup
with Baby Mozzarella and Basil

This eternally popular soup wasn't originally made for the restaurant: it was a staple of the outside catering business. Mark Hix says we must have served it a thousand times before it finally appeared on the menu. It was an immediate success. It is simple to make but don't be tempted to use anything other than ripe plum tomatoes or other well-flavoured ones. It is an intensely flavoured soup and therefore served in small quantities.

500 g ripe plum or other well-flavoured tomatoes, halved and seeded	**For the Garnish**
	150 g mozzarella cheese
500 g cherry tomatoes	(baby ones if possible)
300 ml tomato juice	60 ml Basil Dressing (page 53)
3 tsp balsamic vinegar	small basil leaves
1 clove garlic, peeled and blanched in water for 2 minutes	(purple and green if possible)
	150 g mixed tomatoes, cherry, yellow,
salt and freshly ground black pepper	plum, etc., cut into small pieces

Process the plum tomatoes in a blender with the cherry tomatoes, tomato juice, balsamic vinegar and garlic and pass the mixture through a fine sieve.

Correct the seasoning, adding a little more balsamic vinegar if necessary. Chill the soup in the freezer for 20–30 minutes.

Serve in a soup plate with small slices of mozzarella or whole baby ones, a drizzle of Basil Dressing, small basil leaves, and a selection of tomato pieces.

Creamed Mushroom Soup

A variety of mushrooms can be used for this dish. If you are knowledgeable about wild mushrooms you may wish to use freshly harvested ones or some that you have preserved in the season. We have suggested dried ceps or porcini as these are commonly found in supermarkets and delicatessens. Once soaked, they can be put straight into the soup with the strained soaking liquid.

50 g butter
1 kg button mushrooms,
　washed, dried and roughly chopped
1 medium leek, trimmed,
　washed and roughly chopped
1 medium onion,
　peeled and roughly chopped
2 cloves garlic,
　peeled and chopped
5 g fresh thyme

1 bay leaf
30 g plain flour
2 ltr Vegetable Stock (see page 20)
20 g dried ceps,
　soaked in water overnight
salt and freshly ground black pepper
100 ml double cream
15 g parsley, finely chopped
selection of wild mushrooms to garnish

Melt the butter in a large pan and gently cook the mushrooms, leek, onion and garlic with the thyme and bay leaf until they are soft. Add the flour and stir well. Gradually add the vegetable stock, bring it to the boil, add the soaked ceps and strain their liquid into the soup. Season well with salt and pepper, and simmer for 45–50 minutes. Process the soup in a blender and strain through a sieve. Return it to a clean pan, pour in the cream, add the parsley and correct the seasoning. If the soup is too thick, add a little more stock. Garnish with some wild mushrooms of your choice, cooked in a little butter until they are soft.

Red Mullet Soup
with Coriander and Rouille

Fresh red mullet is always preferable but this recipe is just as successful with frozen.

1 kg red mullet
1 large onion, peeled and roughly chopped
1 leek, trimmed, washed and roughly chopped
1 small fennel bulb, trimmed and roughly chopped
1 red pepper, seeded and roughly chopped
6 cloves garlic, peeled and chopped
1 medium potato, peeled and roughly chopped
50 ml olive oil
pinch of saffron strands *or* $^1/_3$ tsp ground saffron
1 bay leaf
5 g thyme

1 teaspoon fennel seeds
20 black peppercorns
2 star anise
5 juniper berries
3 tbsp tomato purée
1 x 250 g tin chopped tomatoes
100 ml red wine
4 ltr Fish Stock (see page 20)
salt and freshly ground black pepper
To serve
baguette, thinly sliced
10 g fresh coriander, chopped

Wash the red mullet but leave the heads on and the stomach in, and cut them into pieces. In a large pot heat the olive oil and gently fry the mullet, vegetables, spices and herbs for 10 minutes. Add the tomato purée, chopped tomatoes, red wine and fish stock. Bring to the boil and simmer for 50 minutes. To thicken the soup, process about 1 litre in the blender, bones and all, and return to the pot. Simmer for another 30 minutes.

The soup should be a rich red colour and have a lightly spiced fish flavour. Add more tomato purée, if necessary, and check the seasoning. Strain the soup through a sieve or conical strainer. Add the coriander and serve with Rouille and some thin slices of toasted baguette.

For the Rouille
1 small ladle fish soup, approximately 60 ml
good pinch saffron strands, or $^1/_2$ teaspoon ground saffron
4 cloves garlic, peeled and roughly chopped
1 thick slice of white bread, crust removed

2 medium egg yolks
60 ml extra-virgin olive oil and
60 ml vegetable oil, mixed together
salt and cayenne pepper
juice of $^1/_2$ lemon

Simmer the saffron and garlic in the fish soup for a couple of minutes, then break the bread into it and stir well. Remove the pan from the heat and cool a little. Pour the mixture into a blender and process well with the egg yolks.

Slowly trickle in the oil, stopping the machine occasionally and scraping the sides. When it is well blended and thick, season the mixture with a little salt, cayenne and lemon juice. Give the Rouille a final whizz in the blender, then transfer into a bowl.

Thai Spiced Chicken and Coconut Soup

8 chicken thighs, boned and skinned
50 g cornflour
300 g cream of coconut block, cut into small pieces
70 g fresh root ginger *or* galangal,
  peeled and shredded
3 mild red chillies, seeded and shredded
2 sticks lemon grass, peeled and the
  bulbous ends finely chopped
100 ml double cream
3 bunches spring onions, peeled, trimmed and
  shredded on the angle
25 g coriander leaves, roughly chopped
salt and freshly ground black pepper

For the Stock

3 ltr Chicken Stock (see page 20)
3 medium onions, peeled and
  roughly chopped
40 g fresh root ginger *or* galangal,
  peeled and roughly chopped
2 sticks lemon grass, peeled and
  roughly chopped
6 cloves garlic, peeled and
  roughly chopped
5 lime leaves
2 mild chillies, seeded and chopped
stalks from 40 g fresh coriander
  (reserve leaves for garnish)

Put all the ingredients for the stock into a pan, bring to the boil and simmer for 1 hour, skimming occasionally to remove any scum. Poach the chicken thighs in the stock for 10 minutes and remove them. Mix the cornflour with a little water, stir it into the stock and simmer for 20 minutes. Strain the stock and return to the pan. Whisk in the cream of coconut.

Blanch the ginger and chillies in boiling water for 5 minutes to remove the harsh flavours, drain and add them with the lemon grass to the soup. Shred the chicken thighs and add the meat and the cream to the soup. Then put in the spring onions and coriander. Bring back to the boil and check the soup for seasoning.

page 30: *Dionysos, the Ivy and the Vine*, Joe Tilson (1990)

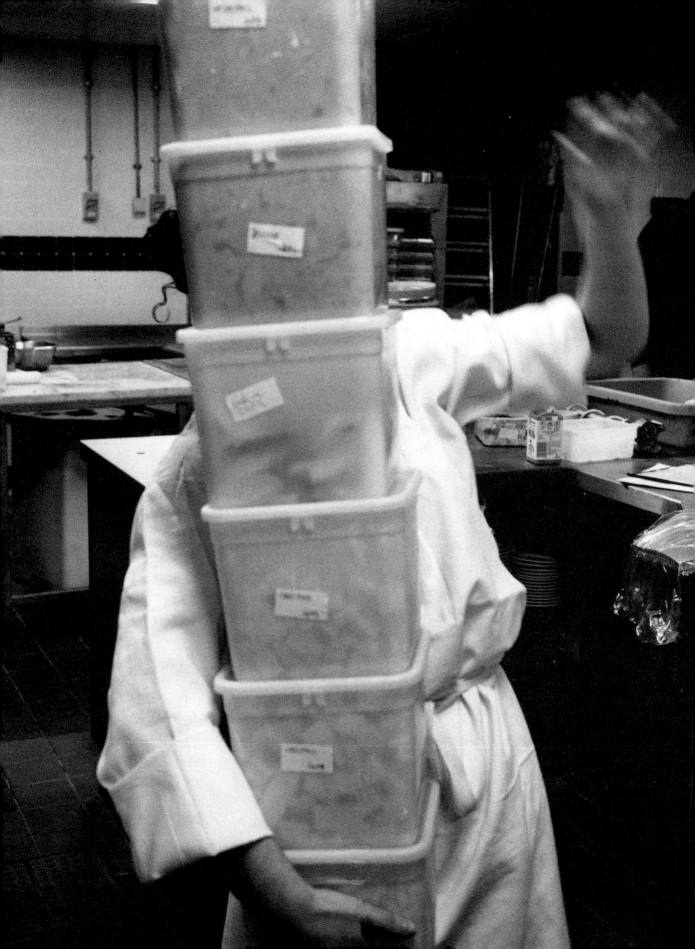

8.00 A.M. The first delivery of the day arrives. Lay's Fruit and Veg. It's a family business of three cheeky-chappie Chelsea supporters, Cockney enough to warm the cockles of Dick Van Dyke's speech coach's heart. They have been doing 'The Garden' for three generations. Bags of potatoes, boxes of squash, carrots, onions, beans. The sous-chef regards an early parsnip dubiously, Cos lettuce for the Caesar Salad and crates of 'queer gear'. Air-freighted berries, perky ingénue salad leaves dumped in a rush by the larder for the kitchen apprentice to sort.

Breakfast. Bacon sandwiches for the kitchen; sliced white, chin-dribbling, eaten standing.

The first Black Suit arrives. A front-of-house manager, he hurries through the dining room turning on lights. Careful, elegant light, emotive rise-and-fall illumination, not the buzzing flat white-out of the kitchen. Coffee. He fills the machine with the Ivy's special arabica blend, the water giggles and hisses in through the filter. Customers' coffee, front-of-house coffee.

Downstairs, the kitchen has moved up a gear. The commis who makes the stock is on sauces today. He stands hunched over his little station, surrounded by pots: curry sauce, dark truffle, meat reductions. He chops handfuls of parsley, tarragon and chervil, pours oil into a hot pan, fries off shallots, shovels tomato concassé.

The kitchen may look haphazard and disorganised, but it is formed, cluttered by experience and repetition - not just of eighty years here, but two hundred years of collective restaurant experience. This is a traditional kitchen, arranged in the old way of stations. Spreading out from sauces are fish, hot and cold starters and hors d'oeuvres, vegetables and larder, pastry and puddings. Every position has a commis going about their small bit of defensible space. You don't ever have to pretend to look busy in a kitchen: from the minute you walk through the doors you just are.

Over by the hellish deep-fat fryer, a big chef takes a small onion bhajee, fries it and presses it, fries it again and takes it to the sous-chef to taste.

> 'Not enough salt.'
> He gives it to me to taste. 'Not enough salt.'
> 'Better put some more salt in it then.'

There is little chat. Curt hellos, a bit of 'What did you do last night? 'You didn't, did you?', 'The same,' and some work, 'Have you got a spatula?' There is none of that arch French hand-shaking that takes the first half-hour of every day in Paris. The atmosphere is relaxed because there isn't time to be formal. Escoffier or Carême could walk into this kitchen and feel at home. Outside, the world would be confusion to them, but the kitchen is the last workplace, apart from a museum and the law, to resist rationalisation and ergonomics and employ friendly psychology. A kitchen remains unreconstructed because it works, and because chefs like it this way.

It's a masculine place, incorrect, unfair, hierarchical. A hard-knock, sharp-edges, fat-and-fire place. That's not to say that women don't fit in here, or are not respected, it's just that kitchens don't say please and thank you for a reason. You have to want to work in them very much indeed to get on here. This is not a place to have doubts, want a view, miss fresh air, be squeamish or become a vegan. Kitchens are tough because nobody can fail alone in them: everybody works together or they all fail together. It's not too many cooks that spoil the broth, it's one – the one who forgets the salt.

9.00 A.M. The first phone calls of the day.

'Hello. The Ivy. Sorry to have kept you waiting. How can I help you?'

The two maîtres d'hôtel sit on opposite sides of a round table in the bar. Beside each is a complicated telephone that flickers and buzzes. The rest of the table is taken up with ledgers, sticky-fingered address books and schoolish notes. In their street clothes they look like a pair of sixth-formers cramming for an exam, heads tilted sideways. They start going through the bookings for lunch and dinner, confirming reservations.

'Hello. This is the Ivy restaurant confirming Mr Vincent, a table for two at ten. Are you coming to us after the show?'

The telephone is slotted into the ear with a shoulder and hands scrabble for the notebooks and paper.

'It doesn't come down till ten to ten. You probably won't be with us until twenty past.
That's OK. Look forward to seeing you.'
'Hello, the Ivy. Sorry to have kept you. How can I help you?'

In the revision clutter of the table there are photocopied lists of all the London theatres' curtain times. They know what's coming on and what's coming off, when to expect a first-night crowd, when a new star is taking over in Phantom, when another has completed a hundred performances as Hedda. The Ivy collects and stores theatrical gossip because it is their business, and also because they like gossip. The theatre has always provided the weekly rep of its cast and acted as a magnet for the rest of its players. Dinner is loosely organised to fit in with shows. A pre-theatre dinner starts at five thirty, then there is an evening sitting for people not going to the theatre, and later, after ten o'clock curtain down, there is supper. This is perhaps the only restaurant in London that is as important a stage as the one the audience and actors have just left. The Ivy and the arts meet each other with the easy, over-effusive public camaraderie of peers, equally famous and talented. Relaxed, knowing eyes meet, sighs of energetic theatrical exhaustion. But the evening is a long way off: there is lunch to be got through first.

As most Londoners are shuffling, crumpled and testy, off commuter trains and buses, grabbing a Danish and a cappuccino on the way to the office, the Ivy is having a problem with lunch. It's not that the tables might be unoccupied. Heavens, no! Their problem is that most of the large tables have been given to regulars, for only two covers, and although the profile is great, the profit has disappeared. The margin for profit in a restaurant, even one as popular as this, is measured in single figures. A table for four with two people sitting at it is as big a waste as the kitchen dropping a whole goose liver down the waste disposal unit. What they want here, what they are waiting for, is a couple

of sixes. Six is a good table. At the moment there are too many pairs. The managers answer their blinking phones and swivel the ledgers between them. It doesn't look so much like homework now as a couple of quartermasters planning a campaign, or those girls in war films plotting the Battle of Britain.

'Angels at twelve o'clock, sir.'
'The Ivy, sorry to keep you waiting. How can I help you?'
'I'm sorry, sir, we're full for lunch.'
'Yes, completely, sir.'
'No, the waiting list's full too. Sorry, sir.'

They write neat hieroglyphs in columns, each line representing a table and a time. The pages are gritty with rubber shavings. Diners being moved up and down the line with their identifying telephone numbers. The atmosphere is casual and good-natured, but efficient.

'Hello, the Ivy. Sorry to have kept you.'

There are two current reservation books, one for the near future and one for the months to come. As you flick through the lists the names grow thinner until you reach just one or two long-planned birthdays and first-nights. There is a single booking for four months ahead, an American who wants to have lunch with his wife and has planned their European holiday with the sort of surface-wiping obsession that makes you wonder if she won't have murdered him before they ever get here.

When you call the Ivy you are answered immediately by the recorded voice of Jeremy King, one of its owners. He tells you that you will be answered by a living person soon, and then you are handed over to Philip Glass, a minimalist composer, who has no connection with the place other than that they play his music for a couple of bars before one of the two maîtres d'hôtel apologises for keeping you waiting. This is as close as many people ever get to a table at the Ivy, and it presents them with a quandary. How do you get a quart into a pint pot? And which part of the quart do you choose? The froth or the lees? It's quite a nice quandary for a restaurant, if they've got to have one, but booking a table ought to be a democratic process in the great English tradition of queuing.
First come, first served. That's fair, but that's not quite how it works. A manager fingers his pencil.

'You have to look after your regulars. If we were a butcher, we'd make sure Mrs Jones got the best mince. We do the same here. We keep a bit back for the regulars.'

'Who's a regular?'
'Well, I've just had a man on the phone, he said he's a regular. He comes once every six months. Well, he is, twice a year, he's very regular, but I suppose we mean three or four times a week. People, companies, whose names we know.'

It's a delicate balance between clubbable demand and exclusivity without snobbery. Snobbery is viewed at the Ivy with the same distaste as cockroaches and wickerwork bottle holders. In a typical lunch perhaps only a third of the tables are available to first-time callers; at busy times of the year it may be even less. The Ivy holds back the rest for the people it knows. Popularity is a nebulous thing: reputations can melt away as quickly as they are formed. They go to great lengths here to keep as many people happy and fed as possible, and once you are in the door, you're as welcome as everyone. The one thing you can't book in this place is a specific table. There is none of that

oleaginous 'Your usual table, sir?'. At the moment, of course, all this is academic. There are no tables: they are still stacked in the middle of the room.

Mitchell, restaurant manager and company director, arrives already dressed in his suit and playful tie. Mitch is colour blind: he thinks his tie is turquoise and red. It's green and brown. If there's anyone at the Ivy you should be on first-name terms with, it's Mitch, although perhaps it's Mitch who should be on first-name terms with you. He is the epitome of a modern front-of-house manager, efficient, unflappable and a million miles from the Central Casting version of a Hollywood Italian. The only fawn you'll get from him or his staff is on a plate with juniper berries.

The old Ivy used to be famous for its Italian maîtres d'hôtel who covered rationed powdered egg with a warm syrup of insincerity, and bowed superciliousness. They were waving, exclamatory men, who seemed to have donned morning suits as a calling to secular service.

Mitch picks up an exercise book from the table. It's the restaurant log. This is a riveting read. Written up twice daily after lunch and dinner by a manager, it's a short record of the service, a mixture of visitors' book, report and teenage fanzine, for management eyes only. It notes how the new staff are coping, any dish that was returned by a customer and why, and what action was taken, which will be cross-referenced later with the cancelled orders on the computerised till, and there are notes on who was with who, who sat where, and what the atmosphere was like.

Mitch checks the book. Then he checks the table plan. He goes off to check the ladies' lavatory. Mitch's life is run to a metronome of checks, hundreds and hundreds of small adjustments, from loo paper to olives, to waiters with Wagnerian love lives, missing ashtrays, missing screws and blown light-bulbs. Bent tines and lipstick traces, dusty frames and wilting flowers. Furious chefs and slippery pavements. There is a snowstorm of paper; duplicate, triplicate, torn, smeared, soggy, furious, pleading, illegible. Mitch ploughs back and forth across the restaurant like the captain's cutter, checking, checking, checking. But for a peppercorn the sauce was lost, but for the sauce the duck was lost, but for the duck the customer was lost, but for the customer the reputation was lost, and the reputation is everything. Like the marginally less demanding God, service is all in the detail.

By ten o'clock the tables for dinner have been confirmed. The tables for lunch have been manoeuvred by the waiters, who in their daytime clothes of trainers and jeans look like a gang of exchange students on work experience. There are four stations here, two of which are each overseen by a head waiter, with commis waiters and chef-de-rang trainees, drink runners and two barmen. In all there are thirty-three tables, numbered one to thirty-four - there is no table thirteen. Theatricals are superstitious; they never know what number their table is, but they are superstitious anyway. The staff work like circus roustabouts, erecting the familiar set. The quiet ghosts of the dawn are flapped away with linen and the rattle of cutlery. The waiters chat lightly over the details of lunch; the litany of placement is repeated over and over to new boys.

> 'This is table three. Where is cover one?'
> 'Here?'
> 'No, here. You count from the left. One, two, three, four. OK?'

The table setting is simple and basic. A waiter moves round his station, minutely adjusting lines and angles, judging distance, like a sergeant major in a barracks.

'This won't do. Get another one.'

One napkin, lap, for the use of, pale green, folded, with the name 'Ivy' facing the chair. One fork with three tines, starter, for the use of; two knives, one bread, one for starter. One wine glass with stem, eight fluid ounces; butter dish, two ounces of unsalted French butter with the imprint of an ivy leaf pressed into it, which, unnervingly, looks as though a dwarf duck has just walked across your table; one ashtray, silver, for cigarettes, cigars, pipes, roll-ups. You can smoke anything you like at any table here: this is not a restaurant that has rules, that presumes to tell you how to behave. Condiments, salt and pepper, glass shakers with silver tops. A silver pepper grinder for black pepper. Little triangular glass flower vases, mauve, pink, yellow and green, that mimic the glass in the windows.

The room is starched and steeled, muted. There is something compelling about a restaurant dressed and ready for lunch. The excitement of deferred pleasure, wimpled, fresh and crisp. Neat, repeating patterns of appetite. It's like sliding between cold, fresh sheets. It's merely a slip of the tongue that linen is both bed and board. A transient deliciousness.

Behind the swing doors, in the no man's land between the white of the kitchen and the black of the restaurant, the flowers are delivered. Big yellow bunches and a bouquet for the private room upstairs, small nosegays for the ladies' loo.

In the corridor between the restaurant and the kitchen the barman checks his bottles, mixers and corkscrews and wipes glasses. Beside him the cellarman goes through the wine racks with a clipboard.

The sous-chef bustles past a mill of waiters to a white plastic board and writes 'Fish of the day' with a Magic Marker. 'Swordfish - no nuts, no garlic'. The waiters make a note on the back of their pads.

The staff are constantly muttered at by notices and instructions. Just out of the public's eye there are dozens of yellowing, typed reminders, thumb-tacked information about fire, intruders, doors, electricity, cleanliness, holidays, changes to previous notices. Instructions cling to doorposts, worktops and walls. Information is power, power is efficiency, efficiency is reputation and reputation is everything. Everybody must know everything, not just his own job, but everyone's job.

10.55 A.M. In the bar the telephones ring steadily. The receptionists take them two by two.
    'I'm afraid we're fully booked, madam.'

Mitch swings through the restaurant again. Just checking. He goes to the four stations of lunch, each like a gun turret in a battleship, entirely self-contained, with all the ammunition it will need: three sizes of knife, two of fork, glasses, water, wine, champagne, Worcestershire sauce, mustard – English and French – Tabasco for oysters and steak tartare and ketchup for whatever you like. It's your food, you eat it any way you want. ➤60

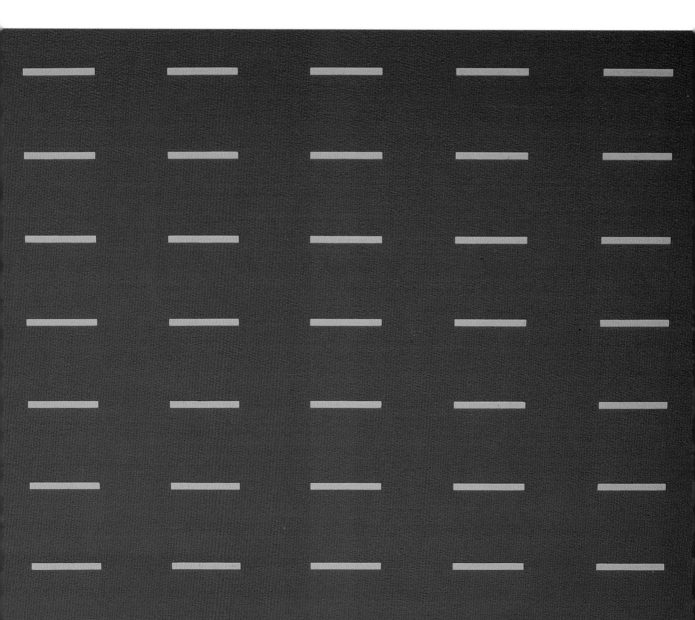

Hors d'Oeuvres

Gulls' Eggs with Celery Salt

It may seem odd to find a recipe for boiling eggs in a modern cookery book - or rather, a recipe for serving ready-boiled eggs, since gulls' eggs generally come cooked. However, Jeremy was insistent that this starter be included. It is, he says, evocative of the Ivy. It's British, it's seasonal, it's from the quadrant of the menu that is stoutly traditional but it helps the guest eat in a relaxed way. He says that whenever you can get the customers to use their fingers you have enhanced the pleasure of their visit. I would add that you shouldn't mind when a restaurant simply places in front of you an ingredient with an added handling charge, then makes you do the handling. It is, after all, what they do with the wine. No one as far as I know has ever tried to improve on the deliciousness of a boiled gull's egg with celery salt. The Ivy serves two as an hors d'oeuvre. From May to June I like to eat them while I am deciding what to order as a starter.

You will need to ask a game-dealer or fishmonger to get gulls' eggs for you - remember that at the start of the season, they will be expensive.

Place the eggs in cold salted water, bring them to the boil and simmer gently for 7 minutes. Then refresh them in cold water.

Serve them either from a big bowl sitting on a nest of cut mustard and cress, with some little pots of celery salt and good mayonnaise, or lay one peeled and one in its shell on each plate, on the cress.

Baked Leek and Trompette Tart with Truffle Oil

500 g shortcrust pastry
3 medium leeks, trimmed, washed and dried
200-250 g trompette de la mort mushrooms
  (if dried, use half the amount)

$1\frac{1}{2}$ ltr double cream
salt and freshly ground white pepper
15 g parsley, washed and chopped
8 medium egg yolks
truffle oil
60 g butter

Pre-heat the oven to 175°C/gas mark 4. Roll out the pastry to $\frac{1}{4}$ cm thick and line eight 11 cm loose-bottomed tart tins. Rest them in the fridge for 1 hour. Line the cases with greaseproof paper, fill with baking beans and bake blind for 10–15 minutes until the pastry is light golden. Remove the beans and the paper and leave to cool in the tins until required, then remove them from the tins.

Quarter the leeks lengthways, and cut them into rough dice. Wash again if necessary. Whether you are using fresh or dried trompettes de la mort, remove the tiny root and tear them in half, wash them a couple of times in cold water and dry them. Melt the butter in a pan and gently cook the mushrooms with a lid on until they soften. Add the double cream, season and simmer gently for about 30 minutes until the cream has reduced by about half. Meanwhile, blanch the leeks in boiling salted water, drain and add them to the mushroom mixture. Check the seasoning, stir in the parsley and pour the mixture into a bowl to cool. Now increase the oven heat to the maximum: it needs to be hot enough to warm and glaze the tarts quickly. When the mushroom mixture is cool, add the egg yolks and mix well. Fill the tarts, ensuring that there is an even amount of mushrooms, leeks and cream in each. Bake them for about 10 minutes until they are a light golden colour. Drizzle truffle oil over each tart.

Bang Bang Chicken

Recipes make their way to the Ivy kitchen by many, many routes. The Bang Bang Chicken arrived after a visit Chris made to a Chinese restaurant in Earl's Court. He was given a particularly disgusting example. However, here was a dish that, if made properly, would fit very well on the menu. The kitchen was asked to experiment. They discovered that you cannot improve on commercial peanut butter. Use the smoothest you can find and, when you are melting it, bear in mind that peanut butter behaves like chocolate. The merest drop of water and it will seize up.

For the Sauce
250 g smooth peanut butter
5 tsp sweet chilli sauce
5 tbsp sesame oil
6 tbsp vegetable oil

1 smoked chicken (weighing 1.2-1.5 kg)
2 medium carrots, peeled and finely shredded
    into 5cm strips
3 spring onions, peeled and finely shredded into 5cm strips
$^1/_2$ cucumber, seeded, cut into 5cm lengths and shredded
rice vinegar (optional)
4 tsp sesame seeds, lightly toasted

NB   If smoked chicken is not available, 5 large chicken breasts lightly poached in some chicken stock for 6 or 7 minutes will do the job. Allow them to cool in the stock.

Spoon the peanut butter into a bowl and place it over a saucepan of hot water for 5-10 minutes to soften, stirring occasionally. Remove it from the heat and whisk in the chilli sauce. Then add both of the oils gradually until the sauce can be poured easily. Depending on the type of peanut butter you use, you may need less or more oil. Do not refrigerate the sauce.

Remove the skin from the chicken and take the meat off the bones. Cut it into 3cm shreds and put it to one side.

Arrange all the vegetables on a serving dish, sprinkle them with the rice vinegar, if you are using it, pile the chicken on top and pour over the sauce generously. Sprinkle over the toasted sesame seeds.

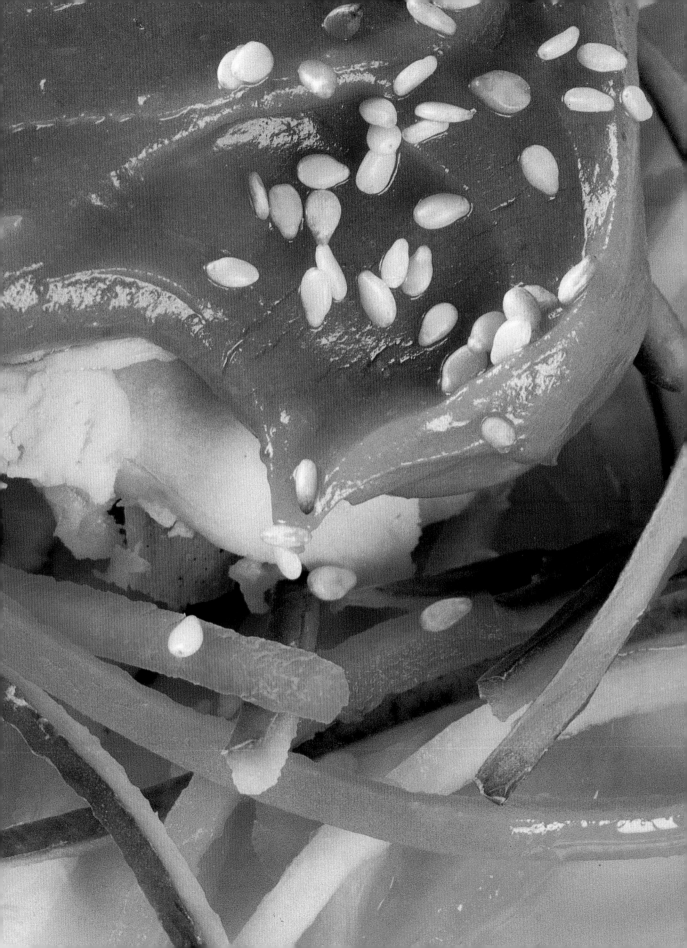

Celeriac Remoulade

This makes a good accompaniment to Dressed Crab (see page 50), an ideal side dish or even a starter. If you serve it as a starter add 2 spoonfuls of good mayonnaise.

1 small head celeriac, approx. 500 g peeled and finely shredded	**For the Vinaigrette**
juice of ½ lemon	50 ml olive oil
vinaigrette (see below)	100 ml vegetable oil
2 tsp English mustard	30 ml white wine vinegar
salt and pepper	70 g Dijon mustard
2 tbsp good mayonnaise, if serving as an accompaniment or starter	½ tsp caster sugar
	salt and freshly ground black pepper

Soak the celeriac in a bowl of cold water with the lemon juice for about 1 hour. Then drain and dry it on some kitchen paper or in a salad spinner. Mix all the ingredients for the vinaigrette together thoroughly, either by putting them into a blender, whisking them by hand or pouring them into a clean empty bottle and shaking it. Whisk together the vinaigrette and the English mustard. Toss the celeriac in the dressing and season to taste with salt and pepper.

Potted Shrimps

Ask your fishmonger in advance to order you some ready-peeled brown shrimps, because it will take you the best part of a day to peel enough for a dinner party by the time you've sampled a few. They will be expensive but worth it.

350 g unsalted butter	450 g peeled brown shrimps
juice of 1 lemon	salt and freshly ground white pepper
good pinch ground mace	2 tsp cayenne pepper
good pinch ground nutmeg	four lemons halved
2 bay leaves	
1 tsp anchovy essence	good quality brown bread

Melt the butter in a pan, add the lemon juice, mace, nutmeg, bay leaves and anchovy essence and simmer on a low heat for 2-3 minutes to infuse the spices. Remove the mixture from the heat and cool until it is just warm. Add the shrimps and stir well, then season with salt and pepper. Put the mixture into the fridge and stir it every so often. When the butter starts to set, spoon the mixture into 8 ramekins, coffee cups or something similar, and cover them with cling-film. If you are not serving the shrimps that day, store them in the fridge. If you are serving them that day, leave them in a cool place where they will not set too hard. Potted shrimps straight from the fridge lack flavour. To serve, dip each ramekin very quickly in hot water and turn out the contents on to a plate. Dust with a little cayenne. Serve with lemon halves and unbuttered brown bread or toast.

Dressed Crab

If your fishmonger can get top-quality freshly picked brown and white crabmeat so much the better; if not a 1 kg crab will yield enough meat for up to three people. The advantage of buying fresh crabs is that you can make a hearty bisque with the shells. This recipe is for a starter portion of crab but with a more generous helping it makes a perfect summer main course. Allow 80–100 g white crabmeat per person. Even if you have bought ready-prepared crab, check that it contains no pieces of shell.

The mayonnaise can be made a day in advance or a few hours before you plan to serve the dish.

For the Mayonnaise
150 g brown crabmeat
1 tsp tomato ketchup
1 tsp Worcestershire sauce
2 tsp English mustard
3 g gelatine leaf
juice of 1/2 lemon
60–70 g brown bread, crusts removed
 and broken into small pieces
50 ml vegetable oil, mixed with 50 ml olive oil
salt and pepper

700 g good quality prepared white crabmeat
 or 3 x 1kg crabs
good quality brown bread

To Serve
Celeriac Remoulade (see page 49)

Put the brown crabmeat, tomato ketchup, Worcestershire sauce and mustard into a blender and process until smooth. Soak the gelatine in water for a few minutes, squeeze out, and melt over a low heat in the lemon juice and add it to the crab with the bread. Process again until the mixture is smooth, stopping the machine occasionally and giving it a stir.

Very slowly trickle the oil into the blender, processing on a low speed as you pour. Stop the machine occasionally and stir. When the mayonnaise is smooth, empty it into a bowl, season if necessary, cover with cling-film and refrigerate overnight.

The best way to present this dish is to spoon the white crabmeat into a 6 cm x 5-6 cm deep ring mould, spoon some brown crab mayonnaise on top and leave it in the fridge for an hour or so to set. To serve, carefully lift off the ring. Alternatively, mould the white crabmeat in a tea cup, pushing it firmly with the back of a spoon, turn it out immediately and spoon the mayonnaise over the top. Serve with some good brown toast and Celeriac Remoulade (see page 49). Green leaves, such as corn salad, land cress or rocket work well with Dressed Crab.

Houmous with Chick-Pea Relish

Mark Hix was inspired to put this dish on the menu after visiting Israel on a cooking trip. He had eaten fantastic houmous in a little back-street café in Jerusalem, which closed when the daily pot of houmous had been sold. The Chick-Pea Relish gives a little added interest.

For the Houmous
240 g best-quality chick-peas,
   soaked for 24 hours and cooked until soft,
   or 700 g canned chick-peas, washed well
8 cloves garlic, peeled and roughly chopped
juice of 2–3 medium lemons
100 ml extra-virgin olive oil
100 ml vegetable oil
10 ml light sesame oil
salt and freshly ground black pepper

To Serve
extra-virgin olive oil
some sprigs of coriander
Lebanese flat bread *or* pitta

For the Chick-Pea Relish
1 small onion, peeled and finely chopped
1 clove garlic, peeled and crushed
1 small red mild chilli, seeded and finely chopped
30 g fresh root ginger, peeled and finely chopped
$\frac{1}{2}$ tsp ground cumin
100 ml extra-virgin olive oil
150 g good-quality dried chick-peas, soaked for
   24 hours and cooked until soft,
   or 280 g canned chick-peas, washed well
30 g tomato purée
60 g canned chopped tomatoes
100 ml water
$\frac{1}{2}$ lemon, seeds removed
salt and freshly ground pepper
10 g fresh mint leaves, chopped
15 g fresh coriander leaves, chopped

For the Houmous: put the chick-peas into a pan with the garlic cloves and about 100 ml water, cover the pan and reheat the peas slowly for 5–10 minutes, stirring occasionally. Remove them from the heat and cool them a little. A good-quality jug liquidiser produces the best Houmous, otherwise use a food processor. Spoon half of the chick-peas into the blender or processor with half of the cooking liquid and process on a high speed, stopping the machine occasionally to stir the mix and scrape the sides of the jug. When the chick-peas are fairly well blended leave the machine running and pour in half of the lemon juice. Mix together the three oils, then slowly add half to the chick-pea mixture. Again you will need to stop the machine every so often to scrape the sides of the jug. The Houmous should be of a thick pouring consistency when it's still warm from the machine. Transfer the Houmous into a bowl, season to taste and add a little more lemon juice if necessary. Repeat with the other half of the chick-peas. Leave in a covered bowl at room temperature until required.

For the Relish: fry the onion, garlic, chilli, ginger and cumin slowly in the olive oil until they are soft. Add the chick-peas, tomato purée, chopped tomatoes, water and the half lemon (in one piece). Season with salt and pepper and simmer gently with a lid on for 30-40 minutes. Check the mixture from time to time and add a little more water if it seems too dry. When it is cooked, the relish will have a nice red oily appearance. Remove the half lemon. Add the mint and coriander to the relish and remove the pan from the heat. Serve it at room temperature.

To Serve: spoon the Houmous about 2 cm deep on to a plate with a couple of spoonfuls of Chick-pea Relish, a little drizzle of extra-virgin olive oil and some freshly picked coriander. Try to find some good Lebanese flat bread, which is like large pitta bread, or serve with pitta.

Plum Tomato and Basil Galette

This is one of the dishes that the Ivy could not open its doors without having on the menu. It is always in the top three as the most popular starter. It is also one of the most plagiarised recipes. Be warned: it is deceptively simple to make and it always tastes wonderful – but it never turns out quite as it does in the restaurant.

8 x 16 cm rounds of puff pastry
   (rolled to 3-4 mm thick)
240 g sun-dried tomatoes in oil
2 tsp tomato purée
200 g fresh basil leaves
8 large *or* 12 medium ripe plum *or*
   well-flavoured tomatoes, blanched, peeled and sliced
freshly ground black pepper
flaky rock or sea salt

For the Basil Dressing
120 g basil
150 ml extra virgin olive oil

Pre-heat the oven to 160°C/gas mark 3. Prick the pastry bases with a fork and bake them for 5 minutes in the oven, turning them over after 2 minutes to ensure that the pastry does not rise. (If it does it will form an uneven base.) Turn the oven up to 200°C/gas mark 6.

Drain most of the oil from the sun-dried tomatoes. Then process with the tomato purée in a blender until a fine paste is achieved, then spoon it into a bowl. Wash the blender and then process the basil leaves with the olive oil. Add a little more oil if the dressing looks too thick.

To assemble the galettes, spread a thin layer of the sun-dried tomato purée on the pastry bases. Lay the sliced tomatoes in a circle on top, overlapping slightly. Season with freshly milled black pepper and bake for 8-10 minutes.

Serve on a warm plate. Drizzle the Basil Dressing generously over the tomatoes and sprinkle with a pinch of rock salt.

Overleaf: Plum Tomato and Basil Galette

Sautéed Foie Gras with an Onion Galette and Sauternes Jus

You may have difficulty in finding fresh raw foie gras: order it from a good butcher or game-dealer.

about 1 kg fresh duck or goose foie gras
100 ml Sauternes *or* a good dessert wine
60 g small currants, soaked in water
   overnight and drained
500 ml Dark Meat Stock (see page 16),
   reduced by two-thirds until thickened
30 g butter
salt and freshly ground black pepper

For the Onion Galette
2 large onions, peeled and thinly sliced
140 g plain flour
100 ml milk
salt and freshly ground black pepper
good quality vegetable oil for deep-frying

Pre-heat the oil in a deep-fat fryer to 140°C. Mix the onions and flour in a bowl, then gradually add the milk to form a thick batter. Season with salt and pepper. Make 8 galettes by using a serving spoon and dropping two or three spoonfuls of the mix at a time into the hot oil to blanch the galettes without colouring them (30-40 seconds), and remove with a perforated spoon on to kitchen paper. Flatten the galettes between pieces of kitchen paper and trim a little if necessary. (They need to be a little bigger than the slices of foie gras.)

Carefully separate the foie gras by pulling the two natural lobes apart. If any green bile is apparent remove it with the point of a small sharp knife. Then take a long sharp knife and a bowl of boiling water. Dip the knife in the water and cut the foie gras into 2 cm-thick slices. The hot knife will help to slice through the fatty foie gras.

Simmer the Sauternes, currants and meat stock until the sauce has thickened to a gravy-like consistency. (Add a little cornflour diluted in water if it does not thicken enough.)

To assemble the dish, re-fry the galettes in hot oil until they are crisp. Drain them on kitchen paper and keep them warm. Whisk the butter into the sauce and season with salt and pepper if necessary.

Heat a frying pan (turn your kitchen extractor on full blast) but do not add any fat because the liver releases a large quantity. Lightly season the pieces of foie gras and fry them on both sides until they are coloured. Do not leave the foie gras in the pan for more than a minute or two or you'll be left with a panful of fat and no liver.

Drain the foie gras and serve it on the galettes with a couple of spoonfuls of sauce around the edge.

Deep-Fried Lambs' Sweetbreads with Tartare Sauce

Lambs' sweetbreads are readily available but not often found in supermarkets, so you will need to ask your butcher. He may offer you frozen ones but you should check the quality (they must be round rather than scraggly). Ask him for the little plump heart sweetbreads, as these are more tender.

1 small onion, peeled and roughly chopped
1 small carrot, peeled and roughly chopped
1 leek, trimmed, washed and roughly chopped
1 bay leaf
5 g thyme
good pinch salt
20 peppercorns
1 ltr water
1 kg lambs' sweetbreads
70 g plain flour, seasoned well with salt and pepper
2-3 medium eggs, cracked and beaten
300 g white breadcrumbs
good-quality vegetable oil for deep-frying
4 lemons, halved

For the Tartare Sauce
300 g good mayonnaise
100 g gherkins, drained and finely chopped
100 g capers
15 g parsley, washed and chopped
15 g chives, chopped
salt and freshly ground black pepper

First, mix together all the ingredients for the Tartare Sauce and season.

Put the onion, carrot, leek, bay leaf, thyme, salt, peppercorns and water in a pan, bring to the boil and simmer for 10 minutes. Add the sweetbreads, bring back to the boil and remove the pan from the heat. Let the sweetbreads cool in the cooking liquor. Drain them and remove any excess fat from them with your fingers. Put them on some kitchen paper to dry.

Place the seasoned flour, the beaten eggs, and the breadcrumbs on separate dishes. Lightly flour each sweetbread, dip it in the egg mixture, then the breadcrumbs and set them aside. It's a messy job.

Heat 8 cm of oil to 180°C in a deep-fat fryer and cook the sweetbreads for 3–4 minutes until they are golden. Drain them and serve each with half a lemon and a good helping of Tartare Sauce.

11.00 A.M. Lunch. Downstairs the kitchen rattles and steams under the neon light. The chefs scurry, heads down, along narrow, slippery gangways between the great burnished iron engines. Staff lunch is a distraction, a diversion, from the main course set for the kitchen, and it looks like it. If you think that food is just fuel to be taken on board so that the body can get on with more important tasks, then staff lunch is probably your sort of meal. Banged down on a counter, bowls of pork chops and baked beans and chips. They moan, but not too loudly – this is not their territory. This is a dangerous, hot workshop, where tempers simmer. They understand that a watched cook often boils, so they don't watch.

The damp pig's spine, unnaturally orange beans and elephant sneeze dessert is slopped on to plates with professional expertise and carried into the canteen, down yet another flight of stairs, in the cellar beneath the basement – an artificially bright, windowless dungeon that contains the staff dining room, locker room and loos. It's a distorted mirror image of the suave restaurant two levels up, the Ivy from a parallel universe. The waiters hunch over the plates on the plastic-topped tables in the little dining room. On the walls are terrible Bayswater Road pictures of London theatres, a smirking cartoon version of the museum-quality pictures upstairs. The staff eat without concentration, mouths open, one forkful jostling the last. Hamster cheeks bulging, a barman eats gaucho style, a long, greasy muscle hangs from his teeth, he holds one end between finger and thumb and carves off as much as his gullet will accommodate with a steak knife, perilously close to his nose. Plastic bottles of infantile-bright pop are passed back and forth. Pudding is sucked with a post-prandial fag, a mouthful of milky sugar, a lungful of tar-blue smoke. They talk disjointedly, through the muffle of masticated gob, about hangovers and lovers and money. Within ten minutes it's over. Lunch is finished in the time most of the customers upstairs will spend perusing the menu. You can't miss the contrast, the irony, of this working lunch and the one that is about to begin two floors up.

The office. Chris Corbin and Jeremy King meet for the first of many times today. They're partners and sit opposite each other over a modern partner's desk in their modern suite of offices, two floors above the restaurant. There is plenty of modern room for them to have an office each if they wanted one, but they choose to stare at each other, in a partnerly way, across the black veneer. There is not much else to stare at in here. It is comfortable, efficient and messily organised in a this-pile-now, that-pile-later, Post-it way. There is a bookcase full of ledgers and files and the sort of technical manuals that you need to be paid to read. In spare corners there is a dusty, frayed collection of restaurant trophies, the metallised tat that clings like barnacles to successful establishments. After the brief swelling pleasure of getting them, they drift off into corners.

What is notable, by its absence, is any hint of a life outside. Although both these men are married and have young families, there are none of the photographs, children's scribbles or thumbpot ashtrays that businessmen keep in peripheral sight to remind them why they work. The only visual comfort is an Alexander Calder print.

Chris and Jeremy have been partners in this business for sixteen years. They have an easy, slightly reserved relationship. A generation ago they would probably have called each other by their surnames. This reserve, this mannerly dislike, is that rather English, unemotional way of showing deep mutual respect. They are a bit like Professor Higgins and Colonel Pickering before the women turned up and without the singing and snobbery.
'We've never had an argument,' says Jeremy.

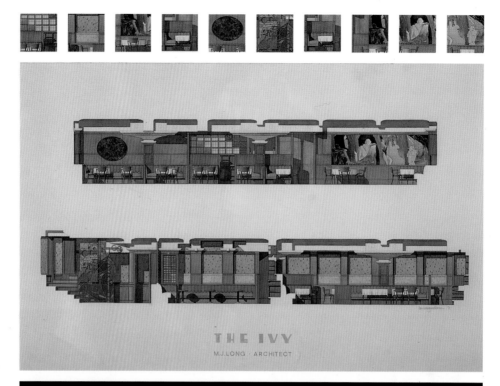

THE IVY

M.J.LONG · ARCHITECT

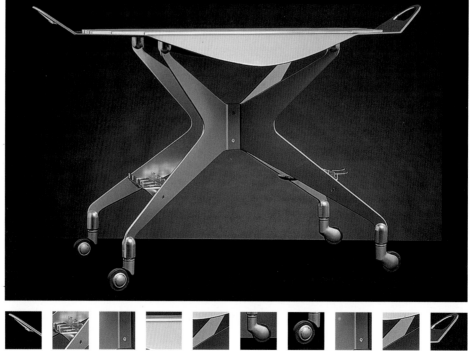

According to Chris, this is because they each know what the other is good at. Chris is conservative, cogitative, thorough and a natural restaurateur. Jeremy is an uncomfortable mixture of the analytical and the impulsive. He does the arithmetical figuring and pushes for change, trusting to inspired instinct. They are that famous double act, check and balance. Chris is a stage manager, looking after the nuts and bolts. He makes sure there is soap in the loos. Jeremy knows how much it costs and how many bars they go through in a year. They are a natural partnership, but no head hunter charged with finding a pair of principals to run two of the most socially high-profile restaurants in the world would have chosen them from a list of two. For a start, they are both as parsimoniously media-shy as Amish pastors and they don't have any of the warm people-gush that is thought de rigueur for front-of-house. With a hindsight inevitability, they fell into their jobs by accident.

Chris grew up in a suburb of Bournemouth. When he was nine his father, who made caravans, was killed in a shooting accident, and he was brought up by his mother. An uncle who took on the role of paterfamilias suggested that Chris got a trade, so he became an apprentice fitter in an aircraft factory - and hated it.

> One day a mechanic asked him if he did the pools. No, he didn't.
> 'Well, you should,' came the reply. 'It's the only way people like us will ever make any money.'
> 'I thought sod that, and walked out.' He laughs.

Chris swears only in private, when he's got his suit off. Oddly, it's not so much an emphasising expletive as a sign that he's being relaxed and inclusive. It's touching. When he talks about his early life the round vowels of the post-war middle-class south coast creep into his normally classless voice.

> 'I went to become a waiter in the local hotel.'

Hardly, on the face of it, a bright fiscal career move from an apprenticeship in an engineering trade, but he discovered something he liked, something he was good at. After college he moved through the various stations of catering, bar-keeping, commis-chef cleaning vegetables, did courses and moved to hotels in London and, as sometimes happens with reserved provincial boys, found a home in the reflected glamour and strict organisation of service, ending up as manager of Langan's, the social restaurant of the seventies and early eighties, and that's where he met Jeremy.

Jeremy was also born into post-war provincial England. He acquired the cold, chipped polish of a minor public school, although he was always a slightly uncomfortable loner. 'I remember my first proper restaurant meal. I had an exeat and went to Petworth on my own and had one of those dreadful sixties restaurant lunches. I thought it was the height of sophistication. I still love going and eating on my own.'

In search of a profession he went to the City - into banking, before banking was glamorous or particularly well paid. Smelly suits and dandruff and stuffy manners. He hated it and, inspired by a popular novel, The Dice Man, decided to trust to chance. He chucked the dice and the City and drifted into bar work while deciding whether to go up to university. The typical youthful float while treading water. And again, as often happens, he found the money difficult to let go.

> 'Although emancipated by catering, I was never entirely comfortable in it.'

Finally, when he was on the point of rolling the dice again, a friend persuaded him to work at Joe Allen, the American-style theatrical restaurant in Covent Garden, as a manager. There he found

Preceding page: *The Ivy Mural*, Allen Jones (1990);
       Opposite: *Christopher Corbin and Jeremy King*, David Bailey (1997)

some magic and resolved to stay in restaurants. He met Chris socially. 'We used to go out with a group of friends after work and try out weird restaurants.'

You can tell that Jeremy isn't good at working for other people. He's a man who will silently look at what you do and know, instinctively, how to do it better. And he might have stayed at Joe Allen, resentfully, until the urge to move became critical, if it hadn't been for something that happened in Langan's.

Joseph Ettedgui of Joseph's frock shops, a customer, suggested that Chris and he go into partnership to open a restaurant of their own. Chris said yes, but only if they could take on Jeremy as a third partner. He's still not quite clear why he said that. 'It was, though, the second best decision of my life.' The first was taking Le Caprice, which had originally been opened in the forties by the then manager of the Ivy. After a shaky start, Le Caprice grew into a huge success. Jeremy and Chris bought out their partner and looked for another restaurant. It was Jeremy who had really wanted the Ivy. 'He wanted the theatrical restaurant, after Joe Allen,' says Chris.

The Ivy had been sold in the sixties to Wheelers, the fish-restaurant chain. They leaned heavily on its fading pre-war reputation and ran it into the ground before selling it to Lady Grade, who finished the job. After six years of trying, Chris and Jeremy finally managed to acquire it and brought back together the two restaurants that had shared a common clientele in the forties. They derive part of their pleasure in the Ivy's success from the fact – known by few – that its apparently timeless interior is, apart from the windows, completely new, achieved at crippling expense.

The genesis of the Ivy's success can be traced to the two places that Chris and Jeremy came from. In many ways it is a synthesis of the old Langan's and Joe Allen. Chris says that the excitement at Langan's during the seventies was amazing. 'It wasn't like any other restaurant. I remember walking in, and they were nailing a David Hockney to the wall with six-inch nails.'

Langan himself was an inspiring restaurateur, publicly famous for his excesses. Professionally, he was also an extraordinarily astute manager. He noticed the atmosphere, read every table. He knew how to create a sense of excitement in a room. Joe Allen, on the other hand, was a dull, not to say ugly, room that got its customers to bring their own atmosphere. It was the big noisy green room for theatrical gossip with easy-to-eat food that didn't put on airs and graces. The smell of the chip grease and the roar of the cast. The Ivy's heritage of Eggs Benedict and hamburgers date back to Joe Allen, and its more sophisticated dishes and stockpots to Langan's.

If the ear for theatre came from Jeremy, the eye for art was Chris's. He'd seen how contemporary painting had given Langan's its chic, modern look, and early on he and Jeremy decided that contemporary artists should be involved with the architects in the redesign of the Ivy. The Paolozzi staircase and the Allen Jones murals of modern and ancient dance are notably popular and, as a little homage, there is a photograph of Peter Langan opposite the ladies' loo. Only those who knew Peter would appreciate the absolute rightness of giving him that particular view.

However, the elements that most people notice and remember from the Ivy's décor are the translucent, diamond-mullioned windows with their coloured panes like silk swatches, which were in place when Jeremy and Chris moved in. Nobody can remember who put them there - they are probably a relic of the unlamented Wheelers - but they give the place its particular sense of privacy and light. At night the paparazzi's flash-bulbs, marking the entrance and exit of tabloid-worthy

Christopher Corbin and Jeremy King, David Bailey (1992)

diners, glow through them as from a comfortably distant battlefield. When Chris and Jeremy worked there, Langan's and Joe Allen were watershed restaurants, not so much for their food but for their customers and their roles in an expanding, changing city. They were flagships for an emerging type of London society that wasn't being served anywhere else.

For fifty years the smartest restaurants in London had been in the old hotels: expensive, grand, mannered, exclusive, jacket-and-tied, sotto-voced rooms staffed by Italian prefects who were there to maintain decorum as much as to serve dinner. You went to these places on the head waiter's terms and behaved yourself. In return, you got to spend a couple of hours in surroundings and with service that imitated grand Victorian country houses. One or two restaurants, no less terrifying and unapproachable, seemed to take their leitmotif from gentlemen's clubs, officers' messes and public-school common rooms.

The cultural message was clear: to eat in these restaurants was to belong, or pretend to belong, to the old, narrow, masculine establishment. It was openly snobbish and they were places that were homely and relaxed only to men who had been through public school, served in cavalry regiments, who were in the professions or the civil service. The menus were written not just in a foreign language but with the oblique inverted commas of personalised dishes: 'Escalope de Veau "Irma"', 'Suprême de Volaille "Melo"'. They did everything possible to make eating out difficult for newcomers and reassuring to those born into the establishment. Exclusive was the word that all these restaurants wanted tacked on to their names, and they meant it not in the modern sense of smart and expensive but in the bald, old-fashioned way of just excluding.

Restaurants were not places of innovation or experiment. They were dedicated to nostalgia, to a time before the First World War when everyone knew their place and, after dark, for most people that place was home. The highest accolade a London hotel could receive for its service and atmosphere was that it had remained unchanged since your grandparents ate there. The old establishment was the only tribe worth joining and this is where they ate in public.

The arts community of actors, painters, writers, film-makers and theatricals did their best to imitate them. They dressed like landed squires, spoke like public-school boys and mimicked the manners and affectations of their betters. If you look at old photographs of pre-war film stars or members of the Royal Academy, they could be so many dukes out of P. G. Wodehouse up to visit their tailors.

By the seventies these old restaurants looked as exhausted, out of place and defunct as the League of Empire Loyalists. London had changed and society was changing. The perception of class had shifted. The civil service and the professions were no longer the apex of an immutable society: the service industries of pop music, arts and media provided a new aristocracy. The media had grown and had plenty of vacancies for new celebrities – no references needed, background immaterial. These gilded, glossy aristos didn't yearn for old-world privacy and civility. Their position demanded exposure and the common touch. There were precious few stages for them, and the tratts and bistros of the sixties were too uncomfortable, the food too bad to fit the bill. There was a vacuum, a desperate need for a new style of eating and showing off. Langan's was it.

It is difficult to explain to anyone who only knows London as the restaurant-stuffed city it is today how rivetingly exciting the old Langan's was. What it was like to walk in and see all those faces you recognised from Ritz and Harper's and the telly, and hear the whisper of polite dining that we'd all grown up with replaced by the shriek of a wonderful party that was here every night. Joe Allen was much the same, glittering with theatricals in jeans and sweatshirts instead of ties and pearls. Most of us had never believed it could be this way in London. In Paris, New York, Barcelona or Rome of course, but it seemed that in London an unwritten law forbade gratuitous exuberance without the Brigade of Guards present.

It should never be forgotten that the restaurant boom of the capital was not driven by chefs or menus, Elizabeth David or exotic ingredients; it was demanded by a new, rich, insecure class of celebrities and media-handlers who had travelled and seen what life beyond London could be like, who wanted to show off their tans or new frocks or other people's spouses, and were just getting comfortable with the shiny, sticky new concept of networking and diaries you carried around all day. People who had come from backgrounds to which they didn't want to return and whom the old tradition and hierarchy would have kept firmly and anonymously in their place in the provinces. People not altogether unlike Jeremy and Chris.

Jeremy and Chris were perfectly placed to see and understand this new meritocracy. They took their shared experience, the glamour and the glitz and polished them till the sophistication shone and they turned into the Ivy, and in the modern way they themselves have become part of the world they serve.

Entertaining has lifted them from provincial roots and engaged them as celebrities, but in their separate backgrounds there may be another deeper reason why the Ivy is the way it is, why behind the scenes it resembles a sort of modern Gormenghast, why there are endless meetings, training sessions, notes, memos and the baroquely complex organisation that binds traditionally transient staff to the business. They have invented a surrogate family, a paternalistic hierarchy that protects and indulges some childlike need to belong. They value long-term commitment because both, in their different ways, need to feel that others are committed to them and need them. All restaurateurs are an uncomfortable mixture of servant and parent.

I put this separately to both Chris and Jeremy. Understandably, each shuffled uncomfortably, but both said guardedly that there might be something in it. Jeremy added that if the staff were not happy, what chance would the customers have.

Considering its turnover, the Ivy is not the most profitable restaurant in London. A time-and-motion man would be speechless at the criminal expenditure on the things that don't reflect in the bottom line, but for the Ivy the bottom line was never profit. This place, the people who work and eat here, are reflections of Chris and Jeremy's attention to the exhausting mosaic of detail, and they have invented a perfect world with the glamour and sophistication that their comparatively bleak provincial childhoods never had.

However, ask them both where they plan to be in ten years' time and they both say nowhere near a restaurant. Jeremy is adamant: 'This isn't the end of my journey - I'm sure I have other things to do.' Chris, more cautiously, qualifies the answer with: 'Well, not as close anyway. I'd like more time to relax.'

As it is, they both spend five days and alternate weekends on the shop floor, but the planned retirements, although sincerely meant, ring hollow. You wonder if anyone could construct a benignly despotic oligarchy like the Ivy - as minutely well appointed and efficient as a Swiss model railway, as comforting as an alternative family - and then just walk away from it. Could they walk away from it? Could they walk away from each other? ➢72

11.15 A.M. In a quiet lobby weak sunlight glances through the blue stained-glass window. A few early revelling dust motes dance. In the cubbyhole under the baroquely Paolozzied stairs the hat-check girl slips off her coat and hangs it on the rail - the first of many. A short, pretty girl with a yellow bob and short black skirt, she peruses her Squirrel Nutkin work-station briefly. There isn't a lot of preparation for a hat-check, not a lot of training or expertise, just the ability to hang. Although she is peripheral to the core business of the restaurant, she still has her standing orders, Sellotaped reminders. The hat-check will sit on her bar stool in the left-hand side of her box so that she can see the door clearly and everyone who comes in. She has to check suspect bags for lunching bombs. Hat-checking is seasonal work, summer is thin pickings under the stairs, but come autumn and the gusty rain, the little dish perched on the lintel quickly fills with silver. She is evasive about what she makes of a winter's evening, but with up to three hundred customers it's probably a tidy recompense for boredom and the gusts of cold, damp air. She settles down and opens her novel; she reads a lot - sometimes scripts. Most of the four girls who cover this job are actresses, resting in the cosy wardrobe of the most successful directors, producers and stars in the West End. The briefcases at her feet contain contracts and proposals for scripts that will play to millions, make millions. Huddled in her care are the dramatic trappings of success, the casual cashmere and tax-avoided furs, the perky, location-bought silk scarves.

> 'I get dogs sometimes. I had a kitten in a hat box once, and a bicycle seat.'

She smiles and exchanges small-change greetings with men and women her weary agent couldn't get her in to see in a month of first nights. They smile back without noticing. A leading lady, eyes blue, hair blonde, can sing a bit, dance a bit, ride a horse a bit, does accents, comedy and tragedy, played the maid in Brief Lives, the maid in Separate Tables and understudied Juliet in Birmingham. She settles in and folds the spine of her sex-and-guns novel, waiting as the hangers sway lightly and the dust gads. Cool and disengaged in the left-hand side of her cupboard under the stairs. Part of the Ivy, part of show business.

11.30 A.M. Mitch passes about the floor of the restaurant and calls the waiters, now changed into their black uniforms, to a pre-lunch briefing. The bookings are complete. The jigsaw of regular diners and a smattering of strangers is fitted together. Late regulars have been found corners. The seven tables in the bar are spoken for. Mitch takes the booking ledger and sits in the middle of the restaurant. The waiters, head waiters and barmen pull up chairs in a rough circle, take out their pads and turn them over to where the fish of the day lies.

> 'Table One,' Mitch says, 'Harry Clorex and one guest. Mr Clorex is a literary agent. He has just poached Stan Dass, you know, who wrote Bitch on Heat, from Dotty Pilchard. I think he's talking a book deal with Guillemot. Table Two is Franny Loggia, with Douglas, oh, what's his name?'

> 'Wingnut,' says a helpful manager.
> 'Yeah, Wingnut. They've just been extended in Mine's a Large One at Wyndhams, and you've probably seen that they're all over the gossip columns. He's left his wife, who, I see, is due here for dinner next Thursday. Table Three is Benny Britain plus three. His TV show starts again next month, and he's allergic to peppers.'

The waiters from the appropriate stations make notes. This is perhaps the most extraordinary meeting to take place in any restaurant in London - part Douglas Bader debrief, part Hello! gossip column and part recipe. Of the thirty-three tables, Mitch knows who is eating at thirty-one. He knows not just what they like to eat and drink but what they're working on, who they're married to, who they're sleeping with, their aspirations and disappointments, their capacities and failings.

> 'Table Seventeen. Bunty Slapshot with clients. Eighteen, Joe Hearse. Actually, move him to Twenty-three - we don't want two agents together. They fell out over J. R. Blackwood last year. So that's the Flintlocks on Eighteen; comp them a bottle of champagne - it's his seventy-fifth birthday.'

And so it goes.

> 'Table Thirty's got a plane to catch. Twelve will have liver well done, but no bacon. Watch that India Puce doesn't have to pass Perdita Dose - they're both up for the same part.'

The customers are as much an ingredient as the bags of spuds and vacuum packs of duck breasts, and they are treated with the same respect and expertise, manipulated in much the same way. And it is manipulation. Although Mitch would say that his job is essentially theatrical direction, tableau vivant, he is more like an animal trainer who gets his charges to do things which they imagine are natural and instinctive. Customers may only be aware of appetite and whim, but, under Mitch's invisible stick and perfectly glazed carrots, they behave with synchronised predictability.

11.55 A.M. Tables checked for the umpteenth time. Telephones ringing incessantly.

> 'Sorry, sir, we're fully booked. Sorry, sir. Sorry, madam. Sorry, sir.'

Stand-by lists are already full. Perhaps a regular customer could be fitted in at the bar, but only after two.

> 'The Shaw-Hirsts' table will be five not three.'
> 'No problem.'

It is a problem, of course, but there is no need to bore Mr Hirst's secretary with it. She's not going to come down and rearrange the jigsaw at three minutes past twelve.

12.00 P.M. The Ivy is wannabe mecca. The media hopeful and hopeless wait in telephone lines to come because it's the place where the successful - those whose shoes they want one day to fill - come. A table here is a talisman for the future. A couple of young advertising copywriters, cropped and baggy, beige and wrinkled, comfortably confident under the weatherproof of their double firsts, their under-thirty six-figure salaries, their model girlfriends, their Alessi bog-roll holders in minimal Notting Hill. They trip in with a slouched swagger to discuss the Hottentot Freshness account. This is a working lunch. The backs of their ears are still wet enough for a 'working lunch' to sound sophisticated, gilded with fast-track promise. A working lunch, to be dropped casually into unnecessary conversations with contemporaries who have yet to obtain the laurels of a multi-media, national saturation panty-liner account. They leave their coats and hit the restaurant, where the smug cool takes one look at the empty room and scoots, leaving two shuffling boys with silly haircuts and shirts with collars a size too big.

> Walking into an empty restaurant is like being the first person at a cocktail party or the only living guest at a wake, but even empty the Ivy is still the Ivy. The waiters understand. They behave as

if the room is full, as if it's positively humming. They don't make jokes, and they don't draw attention to the unavoidable, unfortunate daily solecism of someone having to be first. The boys get to the safety of their table, do the drinks thing and start to talk - too fast, one too loud, the other whispering. It's the same conversation they had in the office this morning.

Five minutes later a girl arrives. Ravishingly pretty, dark hair tied back, in a rip-off suit that looks like Gucci. The rest of her wardrobe is on the bedroom floor in the flat in Clapham she shares with another actress. She's here to meet a director. In her bag is a script, excitedly scored with orange highlighter. It's a part she'd be perfect for - better than perfect, that she was born for. Two weeks' filming in Florence, and the nudity is no problem. Heck, who even has an opinion on nudity these days? She'd take off her clothes right here and now without blinking a nipple, except that it took her three hours to get them all on. She's twenty minutes early and nervous as a gun dog. Mitch understands. He also knows that the director has lunched three identical girls here this week and that the part will probably go to his girlfriend, who's also small and dark with expensive breasts. He sits her in the bar and takes an order for drinks. Her synapses scream for vodka straight, hold the glass, but four years of RADA say white wine. The prayed-over script pokes from her bag, but you can't read a script in the Ivy, it's too uncool. Mitch brings an early edition of the Evening Standard. They keep six under the counter at the door, just in case. The Ivy is one of the few restaurants in London where a single girl can sit in the bar without feeling she's on the menu.

A theatrical dame arrives with her son and his girlfriend. She shepherds the ingénues with one hand and the other is outstretched to whichever of the managers is nearest. This is 'her place'. 'Practically my dining room, darling. Lord, I'd hate to think how long I've been coming here.'

> She'd hate you to think too hard about it even more.
> 'I was here with Rex when I was seventeen. It was quite different then.'

The manager moves ahead like a herald, the children part and hang back, the dame pauses for the merest second and then makes her entrance. The audience may only be two aspiring advertising executives and a few waiters who've seen it all before, but they're still the public.

> 'We owe it to them, dear.'
> The dame has done this so often for so long that it's a reflex, as it is to the Ivy.

The entrance to the restaurant isn't a matter of happenstance. It has been carefully orchestrated, worked out, thought about. You're met at the door. You enter a hall. There you get rid of your coat. This is Wardrobe - you don't have to prepare in the restaurant. There is even a discreet smoked mirror for last-minute adjustments. Then you process through a double door into the bar, shielded from the dining room proper by a screen. You are aware of it, but you can't be seen. This is the wings. You pick up your retinue and a manager, check your fly, take a deep breath and step on stage. Nobody walks into this dining room unprepared, with their bracelet caught in the arm of their coat.

Everyone who eats here regularly thinks they know where the power tables are. One, they think, is the large round table in the centre where the first-night parties sit. Perhaps, but it doesn't exist at lunch - it's just a table top rolled on for the evening. At lunch perhaps it's the banquettes ahead of you and to the immediate right where the television arts presenters lounge. The uninformed may believe the uncoolest tables, 'Siberia', are in the far corner, as far from the entrance as you can get. This is not how it looks to the restaurant. These tables at the far end of the room, on the last

station, are kept for people who have hard-nosed negotiations to do, who eat Caesar Salad and talk turkey. They tend not to be the household faces. Stars come here to celebrate business, but their accountants, agents and business managers come to do business.

The caress of manipulation doesn't stop at the table. The practised second-guessing. Heavens, no! The Ivy know how you should sit. Couples here on dates or patching rows, considering bedrooms or celebrating years, should be sat side by side or at right angles. This is more intimate, more together, than opposite. Opposite is for strangers, negotiators or colleagues. A table for three is complicated. If two of the three are married or work together it may be natural to place the singleton between them, but that's all wrong. He'll spend his time swivelling his head, like it's the Centre Court. Partners generally socialise as a unit, so you sit them opposite the singleton. That way he gets the attention of both. If you've eaten at the Ivy and you think that this is nonsense, that's because they're very, very good at it and you've never noticed. Oh, and ladies sit with their backs to the wall, facing into the room, but you knew that anyway.

After the diners have been seated and flapped the napkins, after they've taken the first hurried, hooded squint at the rest of the room, they're confronted by two things. Perhaps the two most important in any restaurant. The two things that do most to make or break a reputation. The menu and a waiter. More thought and concentrated effort have gone into these two things than into any other. The waiter is probably a man, though not necessarily. He may be French, he may be gay, but not necessarily. What he will be, necessarily, is neatly turned out in a black waistcoat, tie and white apron.

A waiter does the most highly trained and demanding job that isn't called a profession. A man who might be a brilliant waiter in one restaurant would be a liability in another, leaving aside the surprisingly difficult prestidigitation that all servers need to master, carrying four or five plates at once, serving in cramped spaces, without rubbing their armpits into hungry noses, pouring wine and sauce accurately. They must be bespoke to their specific dining room.

The Ivy is a contemporary mix of plated and silver service - that is, some dishes come ready to eat from the kitchen and some need to be finished at the table. It's not just how your waiter does this, it's the manner in which he does it. For many a customer, just having got here is a triumph of organisation, planning and wish fulfilment. A table at the Ivy is an achievement, a personal perk, a small measure of professional and social success, and he doesn't need to be confronted by a bloke who behaves like a Hapsburg majordomo or put down and intimidated by a sneering flunkey. But then this isn't some local bistro either, some how-ya-doin' diner. The customer doesn't want his achievement, his place at the cultural top table, belittled by an over-familiar drama student paying for his tuition with 'Hi, I'm Chuck'. He doesn't want some flirtatious Antipodean dabbing Chablis off his date's cleavage and sitting at the table to take his order. Hitting just the right note of efficient servility with that soupçon of relaxed camaraderie is tricky enough. It's doubly tricky when the restaurant is packed, there are forty main courses due at the same time, the kitchen is screaming like a Robin Reliant going uphill in first and the swordfish is off. In fact, it's so tricky, so deeply complex and fraught, that the Ivy have written a manual about it.

There are training manuals for almost every position in the restaurant - there is even one on how to answer the phones. The rules are designed to appear as if there are no rules. Good service is like good manners: if you notice them they are not that good.

On top of the needs, desires and appetites of the customers, the waiter has to remember dozens of tiny instructions from the management. He mustn't point directions to customers, for this informs the room that they are new; he should talk to the customers but never about the customers; and gossip is strictly forbidden, even if it is benign. The Ivy doesn't allow customers to take photographs and it certainly doesn't allow stripograms, singing telegrams or men dressed as gorillas - unless they've booked tables. Then you can come dressed as whatever you like.

They don't make birthday cakes. They will put 'Happy Birthday' and your name in chocolate on your pudding plate, and they comp champagne. Lots and lots of champagne: for anniversaries, successful runs, book launches, opening nights and engagements. Bouquets of flowers arrive for every service. Lots and lots of couples get engaged at the Ivy. It has divorces too - plenty of stretched and distorted good intentions finally snap at the Ivy. One couple even had the Ivy written into their divorce settlement. She got it, he got Le Caprice. This dining room is 'our place' for thousands of couples. It's where they met or where they came on a first date, where they brought their prospective in-laws to meet each other. At every service you can see tables marking the milestones of life with Tomato Galette and Truffle Risotto and popped corks.

A waiter looks at a dining room and sees it in a completely different way from a customer. The customer sees pretty girls with ugly men, a table of blokes laughing too loudly, a woman who mistakenly imagines that a purple shirt goes with her dyed red hair, how much better a movie star looks in real life. The customer notices the buzz, the smell, the noise, the atmosphere, the theatre. But a waiter is a stage manager: he knows the performance by heart. He sees a room full of plates and glasses, half empty, half full, courses finishing, starting, cutlery, condiments, cream, custard, napkins, ashtrays, bread baskets, butter dishes, the hundreds of small additions and subtractions that demand continuous attention. A four-minute wait for the mustard or another bottle of wine is infuriating beyond endurance for a customer, but to the waiter it has to be slotted into a list that makes an air-traffic controller's look like a piece of cake. Whenever I see those men in variety shows who spin empty plates on sticks with big grins, I always think that within half a mile there are probably a dozen waiters doing things that are far more impressive - and they feed the audience at the same time.

Lunch comes all at once. The evening service is staggered, but at lunch the whole restaurant wants to be served between one and one thirty. There is no special lunch menu; the work is frantic but must appear calm. The most commonly used metaphor for a restaurant is the one about the swan gliding nonchalantly on the surface but paddling like hell below the water line. ➤92

Salads

Belgian Endive Salad
with Pommery Mustard Dressing

16 heads Belgian endive (chicory)
2 tbsp grain mustard
1 tbsp Dijon mustard
50 ml white wine vinegar
$^1/_2$ tbsp clear honey

150 ml extra-virgin olive oil
    mixed with 150 ml vegetable oil
salt and freshly ground black pepper

Cut the bottoms off the Belgian endive and remove any discoloured leaves. Separate the leaves and wash them if necessary. In a blender, process together the two mustards, the white wine vinegar and the honey. Gradually add in the oils until emulsified and season. Toss the leaves in the dressing and serve the salad either in individual bowls or arranged on a plate.

Green Herb Salad

A variety of lettuces and herbs can be used for this salad, depending on availability: Cos hearts, Little Gems, rocket, watercress, corn salad, chives, chervil, tarragon leaves, etc. The secret is in the dressing.

200 ml extra-virgin olive oil
2 cloves garlic, peeled
tarragon stalks (if using leaves in the salad) or tarragon sprigs
juice of 1 lemon
30 ml white wine vinegar
salt and freshly ground black pepper

300-400 g mixed salad and herb leaves

Make the dressing at least a day before you plan to use it. Put the olive oil, garlic, tarragon, lemon juice and white wine vinegar into a bowl, season to taste and mix well. Cover it and leave it at room temperature.
Wash and spin or dry the salad and herb leaves.
Strain the dressing and whisk it. Check the seasoning and dress the leaves.

Caesar Salad

For a dish that is barely a generation old, this one raises more argument than any other. People who cannot tell the difference between a halibut and an anchovy have a religious certainty about how this simple salad should be made. Americans regularly use the Caesar salad as the measure of a restaurant. The controversy about the right way to go about it has led the Ivy to stipulate the type of lettuce used. I insisted that it should be Cos, Chris vehemently said Romaine. I looked it up and found that they are the same thing. I still think the size of the croûtons is too big. Jeremy disagrees and we once spent a happy lunch drawing what we considered the ideal cube on napkins. Whoever's right, the Ivy's Caesar Salad is perennially one of its top three most popular starters. I think, despite the croûtons, it's the best in London but I don't want to argue about it.

300 ml good mayonnaise
juice of 1 lemon
4 garlic cloves, peeled and crushed
16 anchovy fillets
50 ml olive oil, mixed with 50 ml vegetable oil
4 garlic cloves, peeled and halved

5 slices thick white bread, crust removed
  and cut into 1-cm cubes
salt and freshly ground black pepper
50 g Parmesan, grated
1 iceberg lettuce, washed and dried
2 firm, crisp Cos or Romaine lettuces,
  washed and dried

Put the mayonnaise, lemon juice, crushed garlic and 8 anchovy fillets in the blender, process until smooth and pour the mixture into a bowl. Chop the remaining anchovy fillets and fold them into the sauce. If it is too thick to pour easily, thin it with a little water.

Gently heat the oil slowly with the halved garlic cloves. Fry the bread cubes until they are golden, then drain them on kitchen paper. Season, and sprinkle with a little Parmesan while they are still warm. When ready to serve the salad, tear the lettuces into pieces and put them in a bowl. Toss them with the dressing and the rest of the Parmesan. Scatter the croûtons on top and serve immediately.

Mixed Tomatoes and Basil Salad

Well-flavoured ripe tomatoes are a must for this dish; summer is the best time to make it but decent tomatoes are available in winter if you shop around.

1.5 kg seasonal tomatoes, plum, beef,
  cherry or golden
100 ml Basil Dressing (see page 53)
50 ml Balsamic Dressing (see page 88)

flaky sea-salt
freshly ground black pepper
10-15 g basil leaves, red if possible

Cut the tomatoes into different shapes – halves, wedges, and either whole or halved if they are cherry tomatoes. Arrange them on plates or in a bowl and pour over both dressings, so that they remain separate. Season, and scatter torn basil leaves over the top.

Crispy Duck and Watercress Salad

To cook the Duck

1 x 1.5 kg duck or 12 duck legs

3 star anise

10 cloves garlic, roughly chopped

60 g fresh root ginger, roughly chopped

20 g fresh coriander, stalks only, washed (use the leaves in the salad)

1 tsp five-spice powder

good vegetable oil for deep-frying

For the Duck Sauce

4 tbsp tomato ketchup

1 tbsp honey

juice of ½ orange

1 tbsp soy sauce

2 tbsp sesame oil

For the Soy and Sesame Dressing

2 tsp soy sauce

2 tsp balsamic vinegar

1 clove garlic, peeled and crushed

10 g fresh root ginger, peeled and crushed

3 tbsp sesame oil

For the Salad

4 bunches watercress, washed and stalks removed

110 g white radish (mooli), peeled and cut into 1cm wide ribbons

60 g bean shoots, washed

1 bunch spring onions, peeled, trimmed and quartered lengthways

20 g coriander leaves (from the Duck recipe), washed

2 tsp sesame seeds, lightly toasted

Cover the duck with water, add the herbs and spices, bring to the boil and simmer gently for 45 minutes. Remove the duck from the stock and set aside to cool. Skim the fat off the stock and use it to make Thai Spiced Chicken and Coconut Soup (see page 28) or freeze it.

Whisk together all the ingredients for the duck sauce.

Put all the ingredients for the soy and sesame dressing into a blender and process until smooth.

To assemble the dish, remove the duck from the bone, trim off any excess fat but leave a little on. Then cut it into 1cm thick slices. Pre-heat the oil to 160°–180°C for deep-frying.

Arrange two-thirds of the watercress on the plates with the white radish, bean shoots and spring onions.

Deep-fry the duck until it is crisp, drain and mix with the duck sauce until it is evenly coated. Arrange it in piles on the salad, strew the rest of the watercress over it, and spoon over the dressing. Scatter the coriander and sesame seeds over the top and serve.

Mexican Griddled Chicken Salad with Guacamole

This salad came about because so many ladies were taking salads and starters as main courses at lunch-time. The Californian-style substantial main-course salad seemed the answer, and fits in with the restaurant's ethos of offering as many different types of meal as possible.

24 small chicken thighs, boned,
    skinned and cut in half
5 large baking potatoes,
    boiled in their skins
good vegetable oil for deep frying
2 small crisp Cos lettuces, washed,
    dried and large leaves torn in half
24 pickled chillies, rinsed in cold water
4 red peppers, seeded, roasted, skinned
    and quartered
20 g coriander leaves (use the stalks
    in the marinade)

For the Dressing
150 ml extra-virgin olive oil
15 ml balsamic vinegar
25 ml sweet chilli sauce
$1/4$ tsp paprika

For the Guacamole
3 avocados, peeled and stoned
$1/2$ tsp paprika
juice of $1/2$ lemon
1 garlic clove, peeled, blanched in water
    for 1 minute, and crushed
80 g sour cream or crème fraîche
salt and freshly ground black pepper

For the Marinade
stalks from the coriander
1 small red chilli, seeded
1 red pepper, seeded
4 cloves garlic, peeled
100 ml good vegetable oil
1 tbsp clear honey
1 tbsp tomato ketchup

Process all the ingredients for the marinade in a blender, mix well with the chicken and leave for 24 hours in the refrigerator.

To make the guacamole, mash the avocado with a fork or in a food processor and mix with the paprika, lemon juice, crushed garlic and sour cream. Season and add a little more lemon juice and paprika if you like. Make the dressing by whisking, or using a bottle and shaking, all the ingredients together.

To cook the chicken, heat a little vegetable oil in a thick-bottomed frying pan. Drain off any excess marinade, then sauté the pieces for 10–12 minutes until the chicken is a nice colour on both sides. Alternatively, place the chicken under a preheated hot grill for the same amount of time, turning it after 5 minutes.

Peel the skin thickly from the potatoes, leaving on some potato flesh. Heat 8 cm of oil to 180°C in a deep-fat fryer and cook the skins until they are crisp. Drain them on kitchen paper.

Arrange the chicken on the plates with the Cos lettuce, chillies and red peppers. Spoon over the dressing and serve with a spoonful of guacamole, the fried potato skins and a scattering of coriander leaves. A light dusting of paprika over the guacamole is a good touch.

Truffled Mixed Artichokes with Corn Salad and Herbs

This dish can be served all year round, including various types of artichokes as they come into season. If fresh baby artichokes are not to be found, you can buy good-quality ones in jars in delicatessens and supermarkets. This recipe may look long but don't be put off as it's unlikely that you'll use all of the artichoke varieties – for a dinner party, any two would be fine. If you are feeling indulgent, add a finely chopped truffle.

juice of 2 lemons	salt and freshly ground black pepper
150 ml vegetable oil	100 ml truffle oil
3 large globe artichokes	20 ml balsamic vinegar
300 g Jerusalem artichokes	140–160 g corn salad (also sold as
8 baby artichokes (poivrade)	lamb's lettuce or mâche), roots removed,
120 g Japanese artichokes (crosnes)	washed and dried
3 cloves garlic, peeled	15 g chives, cut into 5-cm lengths
5 g thyme	15 g chervil, leaves picked and washed

Take a large bowl and put into it the juice of 2 lemons, 1½ litres of water and 50 ml of the vegetable oil. With a sharp serrated knife cut the stalks off the globe artichokes then cut through the leaves 5 cm from the base. Turn the artichoke on its side and cut away the outer leaves to reveal the flesh. With a smaller sharp knife, cut the green leafy bits from the base to make a saucer shape. (It will take a few artichokes to perfect this but you won't forget how to do it for next time.) Plunge the artichokes immediately into the acidulated water. Peel the Jerusalem artichokes as you would potatoes, discarding the knobbly bits. Put them into the acidulated water. If you are lucky enough to find baby artichokes, cut 1 cm off the top, carefully peel the stalk and remove a few of the outer leaves by pulling them out with your fingers. Put the globe artichokes into a pan with the baby artichokes, cover with the acidulated water, add the garlic and thyme, season with salt and pepper, bring to the boil and simmer for 10–15 minutes or until they are tender (test with the point of a knife). Put the artichokes into a bowl with a little of the cooking liquor to cool.

Cook the Jerusalem artichokes in the same liquor for 10–12 minutes, test with a knife and leave them in the liquor to cool. If you are using the Japanese artichokes, cut the ends off if they are dry, otherwise cook them whole in the same liquor for 1 minute and refresh them in cold water. Once the artichokes are cool, prepare the globe artichokes by scooping out the thistle-like centre with a spoon and return them to the liquor until required.

Slice the globe and Jerusalem artichokes, halve the baby artichokes and leave the Japanese artichokes whole. Make the dressing by whisking together the truffle oil, (the finely chopped truffle, if using) and the balsamic vinegar, and season. Mix the artichokes together and marinate them in a little of the dressing at room temperature.

To assemble the salad, spoon the artichokes on to the plates, arrange four or five heads of corn salad on them, dress lightly with the truffle vinaigrette, and scatter over the chervil and chives.

Pousse Spinach and Roquefort Salad

This is a pretty self-explanatory dish but the Roquefort is essential. Do not use any other cheese. Roquefort and pousse are a marriage made in heaven. Don't expect anyone to be fooled by lookalikes.

225 g Roquefort cheese
200 ml Vinaigrette (see page 49)
80 g pine nuts, toasted
4 ripe avocados, peeled, stoned and sliced
salt and freshly ground black pepper
250 g baby spinach, or pousse, stalks removed, washed and dried

Chill half of the Roquefort, then grate it on to a flat tray, spread it out and put it into the freezer until required. Process the remaining cheese with the vinaigrette in the blender.

To serve, arrange some avocado slices in a pile in the middle of each plate, and season. Toss the spinach leaves in a little of the dressing and divide them between the plates. Drizzle a little more dressing on the leaves, then scatter over the pine nuts and the grated Roquefort.

Rocket and Parmesan Salad

Buying good-quality rocket is not easy: supermarkets tend to sell it in small packets as a herb, and it is normally limp. Ask your greengrocer to get you some or, better still, grow it yourself. Every time you cut it, it grows again and becomes hotter.

400 g rocket, washed, dried, long stalks removed
150 g Reggiano Parmesan

For the Balsamic Dressing
200 ml extra-virgin olive oil
50 ml balsamic vinegar
salt and freshly ground black pepper

Whisk together the olive oil and balsamic vinegar and season. Lightly toss the rocket leaves with the dressing. Then, with a peeler or sharp knife, shave the Parmesan on to the salad.

1.20 P.M. In the kitchen there is a problem. A log jam. A Bang-Bang Chicken and Caesar Salad jam. When a waiter takes an order he first writes it in his book and then types it into the Remanco computerised till. There are four, one in each station in the dining room. Remanco is the great unknown and unsung hero of restaurants, a computer system that separates orders into parts, remembers them, lists them, correlates them and generally makes itself Mr Indispensable. It spits out slips of paper from a ticker-tape machine at each station downstairs in the kitchen.

The chef stands in the centre of the kitchen with the complete order and shouts it out so that everyone can synchronise. The sous-chefs bark back that they have understood. The chef is a big man, an imposing, frightening man with a cropped head, a man who doesn't smile with any sense that this is a familiar contortion for his impact-resistant face. In the nineteenth century Escoffier said that being a commanding figure was a prerequisite for the chef, and Machiavelli mentioned that if a prince couldn't be loved, then it was better that he be feared. Machiavelli wrote the original book of rules for kitchens. There may be lovable chefs, but I've yet to meet one at work.

The chef's work-station is called the 'Pass', is a brightly lit hatch in the middle of the kitchen. Every dish must go through the Pass to be checked before it's sent to the table. The commis- and sous-chefs may make it, but it is the head chef's reputation that goes through the swing doors and the restaurant's reputation that reaches the table, and reputation is everything.

Because the kitchen is a floor below the dining room, the food is delivered to the waiters by a runner. The runners are dressed in black polo shirts and white aprons to denote that they work between this boiling Hades and the public world. From the Pass the plates go to the counter, where the runners wipe spots of sauce and garnish from their margins, put them on black oval trays the size of a fat five-year-old, hoist these on to their shoulders and run through the kitchen up flights of worn stairs, shouting 'Backs! Backs!', and through the swing doors, where their cadence drops to a smart stroll and the waiters take over.

'My greyhounds' the chef calls them. Although the runner is the junior member of the kitchen team, the chef treats them with something close to respect. He can make a commis of any turnip-headed lout with two hands, but good runners are rare. They stand panting by the Pass, wiping rivulets of sweat from their temples.

A trainee commis, in pristine whites and a high toque, stands in a corner watching the service. Tomorrow he will start for real. His face pasty, his eyes dark, he is trying to take everything in, and he swallows a lot. Your first day in a kitchen is the most terrifying of your life. There is no easy way of doing it, no quiet corner where you can learn the ropes to build your confidence. You have to hit the slippery ground sprinting. Kitchens only have one speed, dictated by the ravenous Remanco.

Mitch jogs down the stairs. When it gets like this he spends half his time in the kitchen. No one else knows what is going on both there and in the restaurant, but he is an ambassador from a neighbouring country from which issue grumbling rumours of war. He has stopped the waiters putting in any more orders until the starters are sorted; he moves some tables up the list, slows down others.

At the Pass the chef calls; sous-chefs shout back, plongeurs swab hot stock from the floor, pans crash. The range flares and hisses. Hot oil stutters and spits, the canopy and the miles of duct salivate condensation. Along the narrow alleys of the kitchen cooks sway and slither, hustling pots and knives and armfuls of ingredients.

'Backs, backs.' The runners rocket away sure-footed, missing a dish-washer, buckling under a precarious pile of dirty plates and pans by centimetres – a collision now would be a catastrophe. There are no pleasantries, no excuse mes. They would be a waste of time. Mitch starts back up the stairs, a black tray skimming his head. A runner turns and brushes his jacket, leaving a long smudge of flour as if a seventeenth-century midget in a periwig had just been kissing his bottom.

Only the pastry section maintains a semblance of calm. Pudding will come later. A pair of French confectioners with almost identical, viciously angular faces and assassin-blue eyes chin-jab complaints about equipment. They wouldn't have looked out of place in Cardinal Richelieu's kitchen. Even here, their voices submerged beneath the din, their grumpy insouciance could only be French. One feeds a small square of puff pastry into an electric mangle again and again until it's the size of a shroud. He handles it as if it's a bride's warm silk nightie.

1.30 P.M. The Remanco's thin metal lips start to demand food again. The main courses go through the Pass and are hurried up the stairs to the restaurant. The room vibrates with the haw-haw throb of men expatiating and women chewing with their ears.

The bar is full and Jeremy King walks into the restaurant. He's just come from Le Caprice on a company Vespa. For every service either Jeremy or Chris will spend some time in each of the restaurants. Jeremy, looking like a benign undertaker secretly sucking a humbug, moves slowly round the room with a slightly stooped, patrician air, stopping at tables to shake hands and exchange pleasantries. This managerial stroll round the shop floor is an essential part of the Ivy's mystique. There is none of the hurried 'Is everything all right, sir, modom?' of typical patrons about Jeremy and Chris in their understated conservative suits and Vogue-ish ties. Most customers greet them as friends and fall into easy chat. Jeremy, always softly spoken, nods and smiles and twists his Else Peretti cufflinks. He has a cat-burglar's sense of who wants to be approached and who would be happier with a conspiratorial nod and a raised eyebrow. He moves around smoothly, never outstaying his welcome, gently cutting off the long-winded and garrulous anecdote. All the time taking in the mode of the room, noticing forgotten ashtrays, empty glasses, fallen napkins. He stops at the young advertising copywriters' table. They beam and chortle as if they've just been given an alpha double plus for their homework. He moves on to the actress who arrived too early to impress the director; she's drunk too much, and her face is flushed and shiny. One too many of her buttons has come adrift. Patting the chap's hand, she's loudly putting the theatre to rights. Jeremy interrupts gently to say he saw her Miranda, which he thought was 'very brave'. She beams. The director gratefully retrieves his hand and grabs a fork. Next are a novelist and his agent. Jeremy mentions that he has just bought their latest book and is looking forward to reading it. The writer is ecstatic that anyone actually wants to talk about his book rather than deals and print runs and electronic rights and begins to explain the plot and motivation. Raising a hand, Jeremy smiles and asks him not to spoil it for him.

It is true that he has bought the book, but he won't get round to reading it for a good few years yet. He lays down books like wine for his retirement - bookshelves wait to fill his crepuscular days in the farmhouse in France. He follows one rule in this daily walkabout. Inflexible, as are all the rules that govern service here, but this one applies to him alone. Jeremy always, always tells the truth. 'I realised years ago that I couldn't do this if I was going to have to lie to the customers. It is soul-destroying if you can only say to people what they want to hear. I don't believe that being a good restaurateur requires sycophancy. There must be genuine communication and exchange.' So he will always speak his mind. Fortunately, he is also a master of tact and diplomacy. That Jeremy chose to be a restaurateur was the Foreign Office's loss.

2.00 P.M. The kitchen's got a grip, it's calmed down. The Remanco still chunters, the Pass is still a traffic jam, but the daily panic has ebbed. Chef's greyhounds come back with more finished plates than they take up full ones. The plongeurs lug the plastic trays of dirty gubbins to the sink and whoosh them with high-pressure steaming hoses before stacking them into the kiln-like washer.

Mitch comes down with a full plate of pasta that's tied itself in sticky knots. The chef has a forensic pick through it. Well, it happens. Someone should have unravelled the spaghetti but when it's busy, well, it happens. He attempts a rueful smile, but his mouth can't manage it. The French confectioners construct puddings, shaking icing-sugar as if powdering babies' bottoms. They examine each plate with an intense irritation.

2.30 P.M. In the kitchen lunch is virtually finished. There are just a couple of tables who may or may not be wanting pudding, but there is no moment to sit back and reminisce, to admire the work of the morning. Once it is done, the service is forgotten. The concentrated effort and dexterity of twenty-one people consigned to hungerless appetite. Collectively a week's work, a hundred years' experience, gone. Thousands of miles travelled just to make lunch. Whole summers of sunshine, centuries of breeding and husbandry reduced and concentrated. The inquisitive taste of ten million years of culture served up on a plate, consumed and forgotten.

Cookery is the only art (perhaps one should say craft) where the less you end up with the more successful you have been. Cooks beam over empty plates. The transience of what they do – the fact that their work is meant for destruction, that the better they get at it the quicker and more rapaciously it will be destroyed – makes chefs a strange and fatalistically bad-tempered group. They sustain, even defend, the Edwardian working conditions, as if the harsh reality, the ever-present danger and anger of the work make up for the ethereal spun-sugar, vaporous product. They resist any attempt to improve their hours or conditions and take stoical pride in the assault course of the training in the school of hard knocks, branding burns, blistered feet and cirrhosed livers. Throughout the kitchen you see little flecks of electric blue on fingers and hands, plasters marking momentary lapses of concentration. Catering plasters are bright blue so that if one is lost in the soup, they'll notice it before the customer does.

Chefs rarely think of the customer, and when they do it is with a sort of dull annoyance. You hear over and over again in kitchens that the job would be fine if it weren't for the bloody punters. Of course, they rarely see them. They make food and it's whisked away into the humming ether above like some propitiatory offering to a god. To a thankless, testy, unforgiving god that is never satisfied. The moment one plate is finished, the next has to be prepared. The kitchen goes about replenishing its stations. The repetitive business of catering continues, lunch and dinner, lunch and dinner for a life-time, an existence measured out in teaspoons and ladles and blue plasters.

2.45 P.M. The head chef looks up from the empty Pass, wipes his hands and walks up the stairs through the swing doors. The dining room has acquired an unbuttoned atmosphere, an expansive post-prandial contentment. Only a handful of tables are still occupied. On the banquette a couple, oblivious of the time, stare silently into each other's eyes, trying to read a message that is blindingly obvious even to a stranger's cursory glance. The froth on their cappuccinos slowly congeals. The waiters move slowly and lay up the tables. The phones are moved back to the round table in the bar.

'Hello. The Ivy restaurant. Sorry to have kept you waiting.' ➤110

Eggs, Pasta and Rice

THE IVY

Eggs Benedict

A truly international dish, this is another example of the Ivy's desire to provide seven-days-a-week food. You can have it as a starter or a double as a main course. Although the dish is simple to construct, the trick is in the timing and consistency of the Hollandaise. Don't try to make too many at once.

8 slices Kassler ham or sweet-cured back bacon	**For the Hollandaise Sauce**
4 muffins	70 ml white wine vinegar
8 medium eggs	80 ml water
400 g Hollandaise Sauce	2 small shallots, peeled and chopped
Hash Browns (see page 161)	a few sprigs tarragon
	1 bay leaf
	10 black peppercorns
	5 medium egg yolks
	400 g unsalted butter
	salt and freshly ground white pepper

To make the Hollandaise Sauce: place the vinegar, water, shallots, herbs and peppercorns in a saucepan and reduce the liquid to about a tablespoonful. Strain and put aside. Melt the butter and simmer for 5–10 minutes. Remove from the heat, leave it to cool a little, then pour off the pure butter where it has separated from the whey and discard the whey. This helps to keep the sauce thick. Put the egg yolks into a small stainless-steel bowl with half of the vinegar reduction and whisk over a pan of gently simmering water until the mixture begins to thicken and become frothy. Slowly trickle in the butter, whisking continuously – an electric hand whisk will help. If the butter is added too quickly, the sauce will separate.

When you have added two-thirds of the butter, taste the sauce and add a little more or all of the reduction. Then add the rest of the butter. The sauce should not be too vinegary but the vinegar should just cut the oiliness of the butter. Season, cover with cling-film and leave in a warm, not hot, place until needed. The sauce can be reheated over a bowl of hot water and lightly whisked again.

To serve, grill the bacon, lightly toast the muffins and soft-poach the eggs. Place the bacon on the muffin with the poached egg on top and coat it with a couple of generous spoonfuls of the Hollandaise Sauce. Hash Browns are the ideal accompaniment, or simply serve the Eggs Benedict on their own.

Double Fried Egg with Black Truffles

The Ivy gets through a kilo of truffles each week. I'll eat fresh truffles almost any way – with spaghetti, mashed potatoes, melted cheese and in the more common risotto, and would be loath to pick a favourite, but in a perfectly fried egg, the lascivious, earthy, immoral flavours of the truffle find an unbeatable complement: the combination is unlikely and mysterious – part chemistry, part metaphysics. The fats in eggs cling to other flavours – keep a truffle in a box of eggs and make the most divine scrambled egg you've ever eaten. The scent of truffles is so erotic that when a dish containing them is carried through a restaurant, you can see customers suddenly look guilty and blush. I like this dish because the innocent ingénue egg lies down so happily with the old roué truffle. If Lolita were a dish she would be this one.

This is a great, pure way to eat fresh black truffles and fry eggs, ensuring that each one has a double yolk. If you can't get hold of fresh black truffles, then ceps or another wild mushroom would go well. You will need a truffle shaver for this dish – a good kitchen shop will sell one.

16 medium eggs, plus extras for breakages	60 g butter
75 ml extra-virgin olive oil	salt and freshly ground black pepper
8 slices good white bread – small	50–60 g fresh black truffles
bloomer-style is good	60 ml truffle oil

You will need 8 large ramekins or similar cups big enough to hold 2 eggs. Carefully crack an egg white into each pot, then drop in the yolk. With the second egg put in only the yolk. (You can freeze the whites for another time.) This may seem a little tedious but separating the first egg breaks down the albumen a little, so that when the second yolk is dropped in, it sits in the white nicely when it is cooked.

Heat the olive oil in a pan, gently tip in the eggs and fry them. Meanwhile toast the bread on both sides and butter it generously. Top it with the fried egg, season, then shave the truffles as thinly as possible over the eggs. Drizzle over a little truffle oil and serve immediately.

Corned Beef Hash with Fried Eggs

These quantities are for a main course. They can be halved and served with one fried egg as a light snack or brunch.

4 medium onions, peeled, halved and	600 g corned beef, diced
thinly sliced	salt and freshly ground black pepper
good vegetable oil for frying	Worcestershire sauce
8 medium baking potatoes, parboiled in	16 medium eggs, plus extras for breakages
their skins, peeled and grated	

Fry the onions in vegetable oil in a covered thick-bottomed pan until they are soft, stirring occasionally. Then remove the lid and turn up the heat to give them a little colour. Put them into a mixing bowl. Heat some oil in a frying pan (a cast-iron one preferably) until it is very hot and cook the potato a little at a time until it is lightly coloured. Add it to the onions.

Add the corned beef to the onions and potato. Season with salt and pepper, a few drops of Worcestershire sauce, mix well and leave it to cool. Mould the mixture evenly into 8 flat cakes and fry them on both sides until they are golden. To serve, pour a few more drops of Worcestershire sauce on to each corned beef hash cake, and top with a double fried egg (see above).

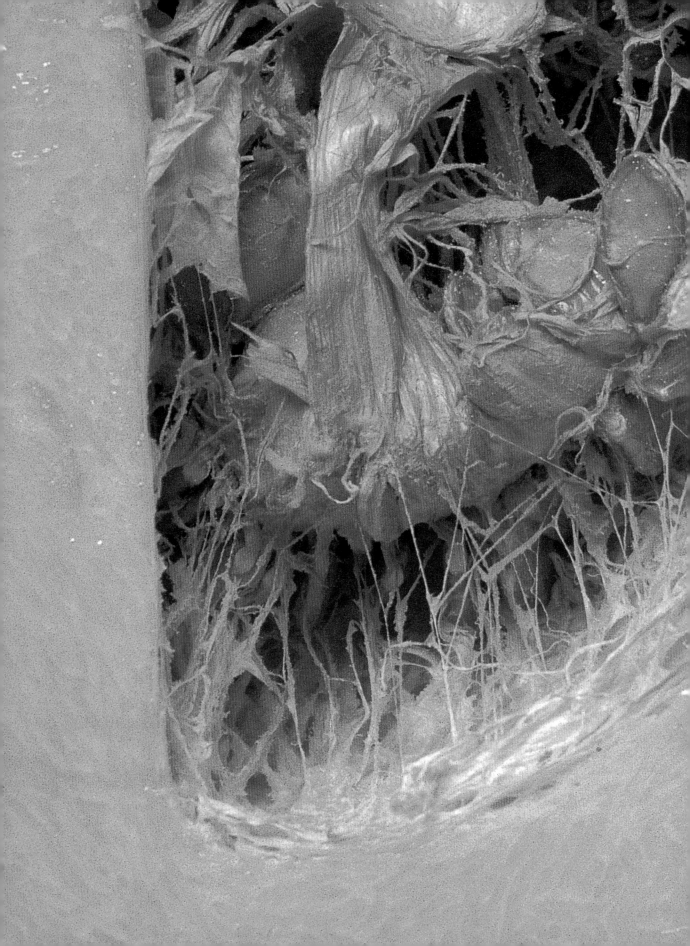

Malayan Spiced Noodles with Roasted Pumpkin

60 g cornflour
300 g cream of coconut block, cut into pieces
70 g fresh root ginger *or* galangal, peeled and shredded
3 small mild red chillies, seeded and shredded
2 sticks lemon grass, peeled and bulbous ends finely chopped
70 ml sesame oil
1.5 kg rich yellow fresh pumpkin *or* butternut squash, peeled, seeded and diced (reserve the trimmings for the stock)
2 tsp ground cumin
2 tsp dried crushed chillies
salt and freshly ground black pepper
800g fresh thick Malayan-style noodles *or* 300 g dried noodles
100 ml double cream
3 bunches spring onions, trimmed and finely shredded on the angle
350 g bean shoots
15 g fresh coriander leaves

For the Stock

3 ltr Vegetable Stock (see page 20)
3 medium onions, peeled and roughly chopped
40 g fresh root ginger *or* galangal, peeled and roughly chopped
2 sticks lemon grass, peeled and roughly chopped
6 cloves garlic, peeled and roughly chopped
3 medium chillies, seeded and chopped
50 ml light soy sauce
skin and seeds from the prepared pumpkin (see main ingredients)
1 tbsp vegetable oil

Put all the stock ingredients into a pan, bring to the boil and simmer for 1 hour, skimming occasionally to remove any scum.

Mix the cornflour with a little water and stir it into the stock. Simmer for 20 minutes then strain the stock and return it to the pan. Add the cream of coconut and whisk it in. Blanch the ginger and the chillies in water for 5 minutes to remove the harsh flavours. Then refresh them in cold water and put to one side. Add the lemon grass to the sauce.

Preheat the oven to 200°C/gas mark 6. Heat 50 ml of the sesame oil in a roasting tray. Add the pumpkin or squash, lightly seasoned, the cumin and crushed chillies and roast them for 25 minutes until golden brown, turning occasionally. Meanwhile, slowly reheat the sauce.

Cook the noodles in boiling salted water, following the cooking instructions on the packet. Drain and divide them between the bowls. Add the chillies, ginger and cream to the sauce. Check the seasoning. In a hot frying pan, heat the rest of the sesame oil, and quickly fry the spring onions and bean shoots. Pour the sauce over the noodles and scatter the pumpkin, bean shoots and spring onions over the top. Garnish with the coriander leaves.

Fettucine ai Due Formaggi

This is a sophisticated dish of pasta with cheese sauce. It can also be made with macaroni or rigatoni, and the sauce also goes well with vegetables.

---

500 g mascarpone cheese
110 g Parmesan cheese, grated
220 ml double cream
salt and freshly ground black pepper

8 portions of thin white pasta noodles
(fettucine, linguini, etc.– allow 70–80 g per person as a starter)
15 g chives, finely chopped

Melt the mascarpone in a thick-bottomed pan with the Parmesan and bring to the boil. Add the double cream and season with salt and pepper. Simmer for a couple of minutes. Pour the sauce into a blender and process. Cook the pasta in boiling, salted water until it is al dente and drain. Reheat the sauce and mix it with the pasta. Stir in the chopped chives, check the seasoning and serve immediately.

Kedgeree

For the Rice
360 g basmati rice
1 tsp cumin seeds
350 g smoked haddock fillet, lightly poached in Fish Stock (see page 20) and flaked
350 g salmon fillet, lightly poached in fish stock and flaked
300 g oyster mushrooms
3 medium eggs, hard-boiled and chopped

For the Curry Sauce
60 g butter
$1/2$ onion, peeled and finely chopped

1 clove garlic, peeled and crushed
20 g fresh root ginger, peeled and finely chopped
1 tsp turmeric
1 tsp ground cumin
1 tsp curry powder
10 fennel seeds
1 bay leaf
pinch of saffron strands
   or $1/3$ tsp ground saffron
$1/2$ tsp tomato purée
100 ml fish stock
250 ml double cream

To make the curry sauce, melt 30 g of the butter in a thick-bottomed pan and fry the onion, garlic and ginger without letting them brown. Add all the spices and fry for another minute to release the flavours. Put in the tomato purée and fish stock, and allow it to reduce by half. Pour in the cream and simmer gently for 15 minutes. Process the sauce in a blender, pass it through a fine strainer and check the seasoning.

Wash the rice three times in cold water and cook with the cumin seeds in plenty of boiling salted water until it is al dente. Drain it and return it to a pan off the heat with a lid on. (A little butter may be forked through it.) To serve the Kedgeree, reheat the sauce and add to it the smoked haddock and salmon. Meanwhile, sauté the oyster mushrooms in the remaining butter and add to the sauce. Put the rice into a bowl, spoon over the fish sauce then scatter the egg across the top.

Risotto Nero

Squid ink can be difficult to find. It comes in small sachets which a good fishmonger can order.

For the Stock	For the Risotto
30 g butter	30 ml extra-virgin olive oil
175 g flat mushrooms, sliced	1 small red onion, finely chopped
400 g red onion, peeled and roughly chopped	1 clove garlic, crushed
400 g fennel, washed and roughly chopped	18 g squid ink
400 g leeks, washed and roughly chopped	330 g carnaroli or arborio rice
1 bay leaf	risotto stock (see above)
10 black peppercorns	50 ml double cream
5 g thyme	60 g butter
2 cloves garlic, peeled and crushed	300 g cleaned squid
3 kg fish bones, washed and chopped	
18 g squid ink	
50 ml white wine	
3 ltr water	

To make the stock, melt the butter in a large saucepan and add the mushrooms, vegetables, bay leaf, peppercorns, thyme and garlic. Cover and cook gently for 10 minutes, stirring occasionally, until the vegetables are soft. Add the fish bones, squid ink, white wine and water. Bring to the boil, skim off any scum that forms and simmer for 40–50 minutes. Strain the stock through a fine-meshed sieve. It should have a good, strong flavour; if not, reduce it a little. Keep it hot if you are making the risotto straight away, or reheat it when you are ready to use it.

To make the risotto, heat the oil in a heavy-bottomed pan and fry the onion and garlic for a few minutes. Add the squid ink, then the rice, and cook for another few minutes, stirring continuously. Slowly add the stock, a ladle or two at a time, ensuring that all the liquid has been absorbed before adding more, stirring constantly. When the rice is cooked add the cream and half the butter and a little more stock if the risotto seems a bit dry: it should be moist but not runny. Meanwhile, cut the squid into 1 cm cubes, fry it in the remaining butter and scatter it over the risotto.

Spaghetti ai Funghi

200 g butter	700–800 g wild mushrooms (a selection or one variety if you prefer), washed and chopped
10 shallots, peeled and roughly chopped	600 g good-quality spaghetti (dried is perfectly acceptable)
400 g button mushrooms, washed	15 g parsley, washed and finely chopped
6 cloves garlic, peeled and crushed	salt and freshly ground black pepper
75 ml white wine	70 g Parmesan, freshly grated
200 ml Vegetable Stock (see page 20)	
100 ml double cream	

Melt half of the butter in a pan, and cook the shallots and button mushrooms, with half of the garlic, gently in it until they are soft. Add the white wine and vegetable stock and reduce until the liquid has almost evaporated. Process the mixture in a blender until it is smooth, then season. Transfer it to a saucepan, add the cream, and warm through over a low heat. You should be left with a thick, soup-like purée.

Heat the remaining butter in a frying pan and gently cook the wild mushrooms and the remainder of the crushed garlic. Now bring a pan of salted water to the boil, cook the pasta until it is al dente and drain it. When the mushrooms are cooked, add the parsley, season and toss the mixture with the cooked spaghetti. To serve, spoon some mushroom purée on each plate and arrange the pasta and mushrooms on top. Serve with Parmesan.

Risotto of Butternut Squash

For the Risotto
1 butternut squash, 400-500 g, peeled and cut into $^1/_2$-cm dice (reserve the trimmings for the stock)
1.5 ltr, approximately, squash stock (see recipe below)
20 ml vegetable oil for frying
8 large shallots, peeled and finely chopped
330 g carnaroli or arborio rice
20 g parsley, washed and chopped (keep the stalks for the stock)
75 ml double cream
100 g unsalted butter
100 g Parmesan, grated

For the Stock
trimmings from the squash
400 g carrots, peeled and chopped
3 medium leeks, peeled and chopped
6 cloves garlic, peeled
parsley stalks (from the Risotto recipe)
1 tsp fennel seeds
20 black peppercorns
5 g thyme
pinch saffron strands or $^1/_3$ tsp ground saffron
100 ml white wine
110 g tomato purée
3 ltr water

To make the stock, cook the squash trimmings, vegetables and garlic in a little oil in a large saucepan very gently for about 5 minutes without allowing them to colour. Add the rest of the ingredients, bring to the boil and simmer for 1 hour, skimming regularly. Then pour the stock through a fine strainer. It should have a strong flavour; if not, reduce it a little. Keep it hot if you are making the risotto straight away, or, if you are making the stock in advance, it can be reheated when you are ready to use it.

Cook the diced squash in some of the stock until it is just cooked through and put it to one side.

To make the risotto, heat the vegetable oil in a thick-bottomed pan, and fry the shallots slowly for a few minutes, without allowing them to colour. Add the rice and stir it well with a wooden spoon. Gradually add the stock, a little at a time, stirring constantly and ensuring that each addition has been fully absorbed by the rice before adding the next. When the rice is almost cooked add the squash, and keep adding stock until the rice is just cooked: the risotto should be quite moist. Then add the chopped parsley, cream and butter. Correct the seasoning and serve with Parmesan.

The chef sits at a table in the corner. A waiter asks what he would like. A pot of tea, Earl Grey. He sits, hunched, his big scarred hands resting on the white linen. They look embarrassed, unsure quite what they are doing here in this room, resting on starched linen. Jeremy and the executive chef, Mark Hix, arrive and pull up chairs. Mark is a quiet, jolly chap, with the sort of face and stature that make big women feel unaccountably maternal. Jeremy orders a bottle of wine.

This is the regular weekly meeting to taste specials for the menu. Four starters, four main courses and four puddings. The menu is the single most important item in a restaurant. It is its calling card, its advertisement, its mission statement. Menus are pored over minutely by proto-restaurateurs, considered through bottles of wine and cups of coffee. The one bit of a restaurant that really is like theatre is the menu. It's casting an epic: many dishes are called but few are chosen. Everyone is looking for that magic combination that ignites the fickle palate of the customers into flaming, insatiable desire. Do you go for a cast of thousands and overstretch the kitchen, waste ingredients and risk mediocrity, or do you go for a focused drama and limited choice for a few big stars that you know you can do well but risk limiting or perhaps boring your public? Do you go for a specialist genre - Finnish or fishish, grills, Thai, French and Thai, French and Californian, Californian with topless waitresses on roller skates, minimal meaty or vegetarian?

The totemic mystical importance that chefs and restaurateurs invest in the grail of a perfect menu is enormous. The received wisdom says that you can open a place in an attic room on the Isle of Dogs decorated by a Maltese debt collector and staffed by fifteen stoned, halitosed Turkish midgets and the public will queue round the block and pay through the nose to lick your plates if the menu is right. Restaurateurs' runes say that a menu must have certain things. It must have a soup. Chefs hate doing soups, waiters hate serving soups, customers rarely choose soup, but you have to have a soup. There must be two sorts of fish, a vegetarian starter and a chocolate pudding. These are the rules that are carved in chalk on the big caterers' ethereal blackboard. There are things that restaurateurs want to have because the public deems them luxurious and the house can charge a premium for them: lobsters, overgrown prawns, venison and - the biggest con in a kitchen - soufflés. The menu rumour mill used to say that even though chefs liked it you couldn't dish offal and then a couple of restaurants opened selling nothing but offal and within a month every restaurant in London had sweetbreads as dish of the day.

In the gastronomic hothouse of the capital, menu paranoia and menu envy run riot. Ingredients go from obscurity to ubiquity and back to obscurity faster than teen pop groups. How did we ever eat without sea bass, duck confit and truffle oil? And who'd have guessed we might survive without polenta?

Of all the things that gastronomic London envies the Ivy for - its regular customers, its waiting list, the loyalty of its staff - the green-eyed plum is its menu. I saw it for the first time in 1990, a couple of months after the newly refurbished Ivy had opened. I had just started as a food writer and I went at twelve for lunch. The name and the history meant little to me. I vaguely recognised it as belonging to one of that handful of pre-war London restaurants that had appeared in grainy black-and-white photographs in old London magazines. The room was empty. I noticed that it was a good room. And then the waiter brought the menu and I was bowled over.

If you see a lot of menus you get to be able to read them like music. You can hum the theme, tell what type of customer the restaurant expects to attract, how long they want them to stay, what the chef is good at and what he doesn't feel strongly about. You develop an ability to read between the

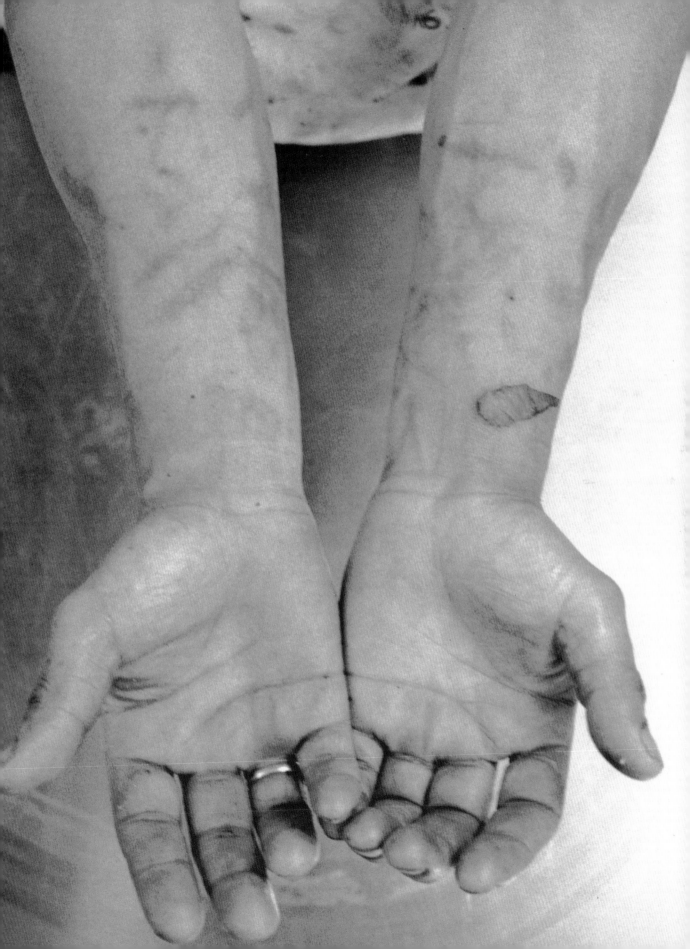

lines. Very expensive restaurants with big wine lists rarely produce puddings fit for much more than glossy photographs. Restaurants with a lot of expensive starters at varied prices want young, attractive women to bring show-off dates (they know it's the women who choose where to go). Restaurants with meat pies and four sorts of potato want lunching businessmen.

Most menus have things on them that are just beyond the kitchen's skill, so if it's mostly pasta and salad but it also boasts hare with chocolate, you can be pretty sure it's not going to be the best hare ever. Restaurants that only offer one fish dish in a field of meat probably aren't very good at it, and vice versa. Fish restaurants invariably have one meat dish on the menu, and I never understand why. Is it because someone might sit down and be horrified that there are only scaly, shelly things in a fish restaurant? Chinese restaurants always used to put an omelette on their menu, presumably for the unwary who were enticed in under the false impression that the pagoda awnings were actually Chippendale. 'Oh, my God, chopsticks – this is a chinky restaurant. I'll have the omelette and chips, please.' Menus that come with a verbose product endorsement for each dish have, thankfully, been pilloried almost into extinction except in the farthest provinces. There are still menus that have been translated in full from some foreign language that appears beside them. I've yet to hear a rational explanation for this that isn't simply vaunting, hideous gastro-snobbery.

The composing of menus is so hidebound and hog-tied by fear and superstition that as the number of restaurants grows, so they become more and more similar. They huddle together for safety, sharing ingredients and methods that seem to work next door. In half the dining rooms in London you find yourself eating dishes that have been poached from the other half. Restaurants flock like sheep to this season's flavours.

The reason I've gone on at such length about other menus is because what struck me about the Ivy's was that it was unique in its simplicity and edibility. There were so many dishes I actually wanted to eat but hadn't been offered for years. This is rare because hunger is not generally the prime motivation for eating out. The Ivy, not by luck but through careful judgment, had fallen on the simple truth that you start with what the customer wants to eat and not with what the chef wants to cook. There were dozens of all-time favourites and there were puddings - glorious, glorious puddings. The late eighties and early nineties were a time when puddings had almost fallen off the list in a fit of fey giggles; they minced on at the end of dinner like a selection of tasteless fifties hats. The Ivy brought puddings back as a proper course, something to reserve space for. And it had savouries, one of the ancient joys of the English table.

Now, almost eight years later, the Ivy's menu still stands as the most pan-agreeable in London. Many restaurants try to copy it, but it has never been equalled for balance and appetite. Taking a single dish, or a handful, from the Ivy menu doesn't transfer the magic to other rooms because it misses the point. The list works as a whole. Borrow the Tomato Galette or Shepherd's Pie and they are like quotations out of context. The whole is a directory of week-in, week-out eating, and if the Ivy has any magic beyond the endless attention to detail, this is it. You can eat à la carte month in month out, and lots of people do.

The first time you eat in a restaurant there is a high insecurity rating. It's new territory. Will you be treated like an embarrassing excrescence? Will the food be disgusting and expensive, or just expensive? You've got to ask a waiter where the loos are and you might be seated next to a sea of provincial, leopard-skin bosoms and Hong Kong Chanel handbags. A new restaurant can be fun, but it's also stressful. Restaurants aren't like the theatre, where you sit in the dark and watch actors in another room. You need to feel comfortable, and it's familiarity that breeds content. What everyone wants is to be a regular somewhere, to be greeted by name, to know which is the best claret, to feel that this is 'my place'. Eating is one of the three most basic instincts and, be it ever so chic and post-modern, a restaurant is a place where the diner must feel a fundamental sense of being childishly safe.

The lobe that deals with taste and appetite is the oldest part of our brain, but restaurants are the sharpest edge of our culture. Prehistoric instinct and modern civilised choice conflict when we eat in a strange room. This may seem far too esoteric a way to describe a business lunch or a hot-dog stand, but the subtle nuances that make some restaurants successful and others fail are so complex that they defy the simple equation of good food plus comfort plus service plus value. The Ivy's menu achieves the balance between culture and instinct. People eat here as a tribe because they can eat often and know that they will be in the company of other members of their clan.

The reason Chris and Jeremy hit upon this cornucopia of a menu is probably because neither is a chef. Again this may sound blindingly obvious, but it's a list that's made for customers to eat, not for chefs to cook. Most restaurants start with a chef and he chooses what he wants to make. But chefs rarely eat their own food or, for that matter, complete meals. So they are often at variance with public taste. The last ten years have seen almost all restaurants bend to the taste of chefs, with a public that goes to restaurants like it goes to art galleries. This is fine, and it is often exceedingly good and exciting, but it compels the customer who eats out a lot to graze over a dozen menus. Eating becomes less of a meal than an event. The Ivy has consensus food, the sort of menu you'd get if you asked for a poll of all-time favourites. It's Melody FM eating, or like those compilation albums of your hundred best love songs. This isn't a criticism – and, incidentally, it's probably the reason you are holding this book at the moment.

The menu is divided into nine sections rather than the usual three. This comes from the original Ivy, which had a typically Edwardian menu. If you ask a waiter what sort of food, generically, you're eating, he'll say modern British. He's been trained to say modern British. It satisfies most customers, but it doesn't really mean anything. Modern British is meant to imply that you are in Britain and this is modern food – or at least not the old food we all used to joke about. But there never was a distinctly British canon of dishes that went on menus. Restaurant food here has always been French-based with Italian additions. Almost all truly regional British food was, and is, home-cooked and doesn't suit restaurant kitchens. Restaurants that flaunt their Britishness are awkwardly translating kitchen supper into a two-star dinner.

The Ivy menu is a mixture of old European dishes and gentleman's club comfort. What is sometimes called 'eclectic', although this is a word that has gone from meaning everything to meaning absolutely nothing. If one had to label the food served at the Ivy, it's probably best described as Empire food. The British tradition has always been to take dishes and ingredients from abroad. From the Crusades on our cuisine has always looked over the water for its flavour. Our pre-eminent culinary background has not been peasant farming but sea-faring trade. It's not our farmers or cooks who have fortified the national pantry but our sailors. That is why dishes like Kedgeree, Chicken Masala and Bang-Bang Chicken fit, without complaint or awkwardness, on the Ivy's menu. It is also why British food has always been long on spices where French food has herbs: the French grew herbs, but we had to import them. The new eclecticism wasn't even new when the Elizabethan adventurers went in search of the Indies. What they were really looking for was modern British food.➤132

Fish and Seafood

Fish and Chips

This is a variation on traditional fish and chips with a minted pea purée. Cod, haddock, plaice fillet, sole and skate deep-fry well; oily fish, such as red mullet and mackerel, are not so good.

For the Batter	For the Pea Purée
15 g fresh yeast	70 g butter
600 ml milk	1 small onion, peeled and
1 medium egg yolk	finely chopped
190 g plain flour	1 kg frozen peas
190 g cornflour	200 ml Vegetable Stock
pinch cayenne pepper	(see page 20)
1/4 tsp baking powder	10 g mint leaves
1/2 tsp soy sauce	salt and freshly ground
salt	black pepper

8 portions (150–170 g each) good-quality fish fillets
good vegetable oil for deep frying
8 servings (150–200 g each) blanched Chips (see page 170)
salt and ground white pepper
50 g plain flour

Make the batter first. Dissolve the yeast in a little milk and leave it in a warm place to ferment. Mix the other ingredients into a batter, add the yeast mixture and season with salt. Cover and leave at room temperature for 1–2 hours until the mixture begins to ferment.

While the batter is fermenting, make the pea purée. Heat 20 g of the butter in a pan and cook the onion gently in it until it is soft. Add the peas, vegetable stock and mint leaves, season, and simmer for 10-12 minutes. Blend in a food processor until smooth. Check and correct the seasoning. Before serving reheat the purée and stir in the remaining butter.

In a deep-fat fryer, heat 8 cm of vegetable oil to 160-180°C. Test the fat to make sure it is hot enough by dropping in a little batter. Season and lightly flour the fish pieces, dip them in the batter and fry them in the hot fat. Drain them and keep them warm. Re-fry the blanched chips in the hot fat until they are crisp and serve with the fish and the minted purée.

TABLE TALK
A A Gill
IDDICH RESTAURANT WRITER

a bit of a worry after
bands of stage-door
luvvie you, so we
Sarah Standing, a
otley donnas, as
ble was a mara-
ndon hotels are
collective trac-
a table any-
You call, you
Not in hotels;
oards and the
envelope that
f paper, two bro-
, and must have
tel chains are stiff
customer-relation
eams trying to draw
away from the under-
waiters, cooks and

much Edward
Woodward.
  Dinner starts
11.30. Let's get
way quickly; we
to. There is an
including a half
that we only al
take back after
let the chef coo
I started with
Don't you just
was an ingénu
balls, with a ta
and a passion
that had shrive
to the plate. T
soup that, if
was quite as
a compliment

Mineral water

I once went to the opening of a water bar in San Francisco. It sold 50 different sorts of water and was the *dernier cri* in chic. Loony? Certainly. But for completely bonkers, consider Joan Juliet Buck, esteemed editrix of French Vogue, who is allegedly partial to ordering a "water cocktail" in restaurants because "straight water is so boring". Presumably, one part Badoit to three parts Evian is to-...-for exciting.

Still, you can't go wrong with...

A Which? report in May last... year found that mineral wat... ...00% more ex...

...Safeway...
...was nice, sof...
Marks &...

...are more un-
...ce chain that is
...ble enough and
...by producers
...up some very
...ns. Indeed, it
...99 wine, a vi-
...ute under the
...hich it hopes
...r. The ware-
...also secur...
...ly regular...
...orth inv...
...ommen...

...had no
...ead, the
...ish).
...ugh I am
...urdity of
...tter" than
S, too, but
...salty taste of
Vichy, although many don't.

India Knight

Waitrose Scottish Natural
Mineral Water
(2l, 59p) *****
Tap water
(1l, 0.048p) *****
Marks & Spencer Natural

---

we'll call you". The se...
appalling, which wasn't enti...
waiter's fault. The other six p...
who should have been looking a...
the dining room were driving hom...
...Mondeos after a hard...

Now, on with...
Barr, trouper on numerous London
boards, a nascently portly chap in a
Demis Roussos-style beginner's
shirt. Just a man, a mike, a stool...
a pianist called Fizz Sha...
"Hi! People have sa...
them of Anthony N...
was not a...
he was rat...
not the sort...
ping centre...e did...quite
moody chat and the...dheim.
well, but he would sing...
All singers love singing Sondheim
because it's difficult and the words
mean bleak, brittle things. Audi-
ences hate it, but this audience
wasn't about to complain. They'd
paid for an evening of old-fashioned
sophistication in Edwardian comfort
...of London's Theatre-

abaret at
ut of the
managed
e of £35,
ouse wine
waiter to
sed not to
ohnny and
of melon.
ade? This
oped into
f ruby port
wi garnish
elded itself
had tomato
ome-made,
ned. That's
like tinned
ove got a

she with a Brief Enc...ardo
and frock, he in a bla...
...cket and dan...
...cters

...d cabaret is a wonderful
idea, p...ct for all those couples
who've run out of things to chat
about. This wasn't how it should be
done, though. This was the Mickey
...version. "Hey, let's do it

ST... RIGHT...

1994 Merlot

Fillet of Haddock with Crab Tabbouleh

Haddock is an underrated fish but, like cod, at its freshest it's great. Ask your fishmonger to fillet it, remove the scales and pin bones (the single bones running down the centre of the fillet) and cut it into 200 g portions.

For the Tabbouleh
1 bunch spring onions, finely chopped
1 small red chilli, seeded and finely chopped
3 ripe plum tomatoes, peeled, seeded and cut into $1/2$ cm dice
320 g couscous
juice of 2 lemons
70 ml extra-virgin olive oil
salt and freshly ground black pepper
100 ml boiling water
20 g parsley, washed and finely chopped
15 g mint leaves, washed and finely chopped
250 g fresh white crabmeat (check that all shell has been removed)

For the Haddock
2 lemons, peeled and segmented
juice of 1 lemon
180 ml extra-virgin olive oil
salt and pepper
8 x 200 g pieces haddock fillet
vegetable oil for frying
50 g butter

To make the Tabbouleh, mix together the spring onion, chilli, tomatoes, couscous, juice of 2 lemons, olive oil, seasoning and boiling water. Cover with cling-film and leave the bowl to stand for 1 hour. Then stir in the parsley, mint and crabmeat.

Cut each lemon segment into three and mix with the olive oil, juice of 1 lemon and season to taste.

Lightly season the haddock portions and fry them in a little vegetable oil, skin side down first, for 2-3 minutes on each side. When the fish is almost cooked add the butter and baste well to give the haddock a nice shine.

Make a pile of Tabbouleh in the centre of each plate, put the fish on top and spoon the lemon dressing around the edge. Serve immediately.

Lobster Thermidor

The true success of this recipe depends on buying live lobsters. Try to buy native if possible rather than the farmed Canadian and American ones. The tail will yield more meat and be much sweeter.

20 ml white wine vinegar
8 x 450-500 g lobsters or 4 large 1 kg lobsters
200 ml white wine
8 shallots, peeled and finely chopped
400 ml Fish Stock (see page 20)
300 ml double cream
20 g English mustard
80 g Cheddar cheese, grated
2 medium egg yolks
salt and freshly ground black pepper

Bring a large pan of water to the boil and add a couple of tablespoons of salt and the white wine vinegar. You will probably need to cook the lobsters in two or three batches, according to the size of your largest saucepan. Plunge them into the boiling water – allow 5 minutes for the smaller ones and 10 for the larger. Remove them from the water and leave them to cool.

Meanwhile, in a pan, reduce the white wine with the shallots until it has almost evaporated. Add the fish stock and reduce again similarly. Add 200 ml of the cream, and the mustard, and reduce until the sauce is quite thick. Then add the grated cheese and whisk until the sauce is smooth. Season and leave it to cool.

Whip the remaining 100 ml of double cream until it forms soft peaks and fold it into the sauce with the egg yolks.

Preheat the oven to 230°C/gas mark 8. Remove the claws from each lobster, crack them and take out the meat. Cut each body in half lengthways by inserting the point of the knife in the head and pushing it with the palm of your hand down through the centre. Remove the meat from the tails and cut it into four pieces. Mix it with a little sauce and lay it back in the tail end of the shell, with the meat from the claws cut into pieces and put into the head section.

Spoon more sauce over the lobster meat, bake in the oven for 10–15 minutes until the lobsters are nicely glazed, or put them under a hot grill for 4–5 minutes.

Serve with Green Herb Salad (see page 80).

Roasted Mixed Shellfish

Choose four or five different shellfish from those listed below.

---

4 small live lobsters
4 live crabs (750 g-1.5 kg each)
8 fresh, raw jumbo prawns (use frozen as a second choice)
500 g large live mussels, washed and de-bearded
500 g live clams, washed
other shellfish such as queen scallops in the half shell, large diver-caught scallops in the
    half-shell; razor clams, even oysters, work well
250 g butter
8 cloves garlic, peeled and crushed
25 g parsley, washed and chopped
salt and freshly ground black pepper
50 ml extra-virgin olive oil
4 lemons, halved

If you prefer not to remove the claws from a live crab and cut a live lobster in half, then put the crabs and lobsters into rapidly boiling water for 2 minutes to kill them, then cool in cold water. Cut the lobsters in half lengthways with a sharp, heavy knife. To do this, insert the point of the knife through the head and apply pressure on the back of the knife with your hand. Crack the claws once with the back of the knife. Remove the claws from the crabs to make them easier to eat once cooked, and crack them with the back of a knife.

Soften the butter to room temperature, mix in the garlic and parsley and season with salt and pepper. Pre-heat the oven to 245°C/gas mark 9. Divide the olive oil between two deep roasting trays and put them in the oven for about 10 minutes, until sizzling. Season the larger shellfish. Place the shellfish in the hot trays and return them to the oven for 10 minutes. Then add the prawns, clams, mussels, etc., and the garlic butter, give them a good stir and return the trays to the oven for another 10 minutes. Check that the mussels and clams have opened and discard any that are still closed.

Serve immediately with some good warm bread and lemon halves.

Roast Fillet of Cod
with Mashed Potato and Parsley Sauce

$\frac{1}{2}$ quantity of Fishcake Sauce, without sorrel (see page 126)
100 ml Fish Stock (see page 20)
50 g parsley, washed and finely chopped
100 g butter

8 x 225 g pieces thick cod fillet, with the skin left on
salt and freshly ground white pepper
good vegetable oil for frying
8 small servings of Mashed Potato (see page 170)

Pre-heat the oven to 230°C/gas mark 8. Bring the fishcake sauce and fish stock to the boil, then reduce to a simmer and cook until the mixture has reduced a little. Add the chopped parsley and half of the butter. Stir well, remove from the heat and season to taste.

Season the pieces of cod and fry them in a little vegetable oil for a few minutes on the skin side first, then turn them over and finish cooking them in the oven for 5–10 minutes. When the fish is almost cooked (it will have lost all its translucency) add the rest of the butter and baste well.
Serve the fish on the mashed potato and pour the sauce around it.

Skate with Black Butter and Capers

Most people are put off by skate as it is normally served on the bone. Although many fish benefit from being cooked on the bone, skate bones are soft and easily swallowed. Ask your fishmonger to skin and fillet your skate – this may surprise him, as it is not normal practice.

8 x 200 g pieces of skate fillet
salt and freshly ground black pepper
2 tbsp plain flour
good vegetable oil for frying
450 g unsalted butter

250 ml Dark Meat Stock (see page 16), reduced by three-quarters
240 g good-quality capers, preferably packed in brine, drained and rinsed
juice of 1 lemon
15 g parsley, washed and finely chopped

Fold the skate fillets to give a uniform shape, season and lightly flour them. Heat the vegetable oil in a pan and fry the fillets on the flat side until they are golden. Then add 50 g of the butter, turn the fillets over and continue cooking for three minutes. Remove them from the pan and keep warm. Wipe the pan with some kitchen paper, add the rest of the butter and heat until foaming – keep an eye on it because it will burn very quickly. As it goes dark brown add the capers, lemon juice and parsley, and remove from the heat. Reheat the reduced meat stock.

Put the skate fillets on to warm plates, pour a little of the reduced meat stock around them and spoon the caper butter generously over the top. Serve with spinach and good buttery mash.

Salmon Fishcake with Sorrel Sauce

The most copied dish on the menu. It came originally from Le Caprice: Chris, seated at the bar, read a recipe for fishcakes in a Sunday paper and asked the chef to see if he could improve on it. The result was immediately popular – they didn't realise quite how popular until they dropped it. The menu had to be reprinted. There are customers who still order nothing else.

When you make them, don't skip the resting time in the fridge. It stops them falling apart in the pan.

For the Fishcakes
650 g dry mashed potato, no cream or butter added (see page 170)
650 g salmon fillet, poached in fish stock and flaked
2 tbsp tomato ketchup
2 tsp anchovy essence
3 tsp English mustard
salt and freshly ground black pepper

For the Sauce
$\frac{1}{2}$ ltr strong Fish Stock (see page 20)
50 g butter
30 g flour
50 ml white wine
250 ml double cream
15 g fresh sorrel, shredded
salt and pepper

1.5 kg spinach, picked over, washed and dried

To make the fishcakes, mix together the potato, half the poached salmon, the ketchup, anchovy essence, mustard and seasoning until is smooth. Fold in the rest of the salmon. Mould the mixture into 8 round cakes and refrigerate.

To make the sauce, bring the fish stock to the boil in a thick-bottomed pan. In another pan melt the butter and stir in the flour. Cook very slowly over a low heat for 30 seconds, then gradually whisk in the fish stock. Pour in the white wine and simmer gently for 30 minutes until the sauce has thickened. Add the cream and reduce the sauce until it is of a thick pouring consistency, then put in the sorrel and season.

Preheat the oven to 200°C/gas mark 6. Lightly flour the fishcakes and fry them until they are coloured on both sides, then bake them for 10–15 minutes.

Heat a large saucepan over a medium flame, add the spinach, season it lightly and cover tightly with a lid. Cook for 3-4 minutes, stirring occasionally, until the leaves are tender. Drain in a colander.

Put some spinach on each plate, then a fishcake and pour over the sauce. Serve immediately.

Seared Scallops with Crispy Bacon and Baby Spinach

Buy good quality fresh scallops, removed from the shell and cleaned. Make sure that they have not been soaked in water or previously frozen.

1 kg good quality large scallop meat
250 g thinly sliced pancetta *or* smoked
   streaky bacon, rind removed
25 ml extra-virgin olive oil

salt and freshly ground black pepper
200 g baby spinach, washed, dried,
   long stalks removed
100 ml Balsamic Dressing (see page 88)

If the fishmonger has not already done so, remove from the scallops the little white muscle attached to the nut of meat with your fingers or with a sharp knife, and briefly wash and dry them on kitchen paper. Grill the bacon until it is crisp. Meanwhile lightly rub a frying pan with olive oil and heat it until it begins to smoke. Season the scallops and fry them for a minute or so until they are nicely coloured on both sides but slightly undercooked. Season and lightly toss the spinach leaves in the dressing. Place a serving of spinach on each plate and arrange the scallops and bacon on the leaves.

Seared Tuna with Spiced Lentil Salsa

The finest blue or yellow fin tuna loin must be used for this dish. Ask your fishmonger to skin and clean the blood line and to cut the tuna into approximately 10 cm long, 4 cm x 4 cm square, blocks: the fish will be sliced after cooking. If you are serving this as a starter allow about 100 g per person or 170 g as a main course. The lentil salsa can be made the day before.

8 10 cm long, 4 cm x 4 cm square,
   blocks tuna loin, weight depending
   on serving size
1 tsp good quality vegetable oil or olive oil

For the Lentil Salsa
200 g Puy lentils, soaked for 3–4 hours
   and washed
40 g fresh root ginger, peeled and
   finely chopped
2 medium mild chillies, seeded and
   finely chopped

1 medium red onion, peeled and finely chopped
2 cloves garlic, peeled and crushed
1 teaspoon ground cumin
$1/2$ teaspoon cumin seeds
50 ml water
50 ml balsamic vinegar
50 ml sweet soy sauce or light soy
2 tablespoons tomato ketchup
1 tablespoon sweet chilli sauce
50 ml olive oil
15 g fresh coriander, finely chopped
salt and pepper

Cook the lentils in salted water for 15–20 minutes or until they are tender. Drain and cool them. Place the ginger and chillies in a pan with the onion, garlic, ground cumin and seeds, water and balsamic vinegar and simmer with a lid on for a few minutes, stirring well so that all the flavours infuse. Remove the mixture from the heat and pour into a bowl with the drained lentils. Add the soy sauce, ketchup and chilli sauce, stir well and gradually add the olive oil and chopped coriander. Season, cover and leave in the refrigerator overnight (if time allows).

To serve: season the pieces of tuna and fry them on each side in a hot pan with a little vegetable oil. Tuna is ideally eaten blue or rare (almost raw) so this will take only 2–3 minutes. If this does not suit all your guests, cook the pieces until medium rare, which takes 5–6 minutes. Once cooked, remove the tuna from the pan and leave it on a plate for 5 minutes to ease carving. Meanwhile, warm the lentils gently in a pan. With a very sharp knife slice the tuna against the grain of the fish into 3 or 4 slices. Serve on the lentils.

Thai Baked Sea Bass with Fragrant Rice

You can sometimes order banana leaves from a good Asian or exotic greengrocer. If that fails wrap the fish in foil or greaseproof paper.

For the Dipping Sauce
25 ml sesame oil
1 small red chilli, seeded and finely chopped
35 g fresh root ginger *or* galangal, peeled and finely chopped
1 stick lemon grass, peeled with the bulbous ends finely chopped
3 lime leaves
2 cloves garlic, peeled and crushed
125 ml sweet soy sauce
100 ml light soy sauce

For the Fragrant Rice
2 sticks lemon grass, peeled and bulbous ends crushed
8 lime leaves
1.5 ltr salted water
225 g basmati rice, washed twice in cold water

For the Sea Bass
35 ml sesame oil
3 medium chillies, seeded and roughly chopped
3 sticks lemon grass, peeled, with the bulbous ends roughly chopped
80 g fresh root ginger *or* galangal, peeled and roughly chopped
4 cloves garlic, peeled and crushed
8 lime leaves, roughly chopped
15 g fresh coriander
8 x 200 g pieces sea bass, scaled and filleted
1–2 metres banana leaf

First, make the dipping sauce. Heat the sesame oil in a pan and fry the chilli, ginger, lemon grass and lime leaves slowly with the garlic for 1 minute to soften and release the flavours. Add both soy sauces, bring the mixture to the boil, then cool and pour it into a bowl or, ideally, individual soy dishes.

Now for the rice: simmer the lemon grass with the lime leaves in the salted water for 10 minutes. Add the rice and simmer for 10–12 minutes until it is just cooked. Drain in a colander, then return to the pan with a lid on and let it stand for 10 minutes before serving. This will help it become nice and fluffy. Serve the rice in individual bowls or put it in a large bowl to pass round.

While the rice is cooking, prepare the fish. Preheat the oven to 200°C/gas mark 6. Heat the sesame oil in a pan and fry the chillies, lemon grass, ginger, garlic and lime leaves in it for a couple of minutes. Then put them into a food processor with the coriander and chop finely. Spread the paste on each fillet and wrap it in a piece of banana leaf like a parcel, folding the leaf so that the edges join underneath the fillet. Bake for 10–15 minutes. Serve the fish on individual plates with a little pot of dipping sauce and the Fragrant Rice or pass a large bowl round.

Overleaf (below): Seared Tuna with Spiced Lentil Salsa

4.30 P.M. The doorman arrives. Glad-hand, Irish matey. He swivels round the reservations book and makes a note of his favourite customers.

'I like to keep a note.'

He goes to the bar and calls his favourite cab companies - just to check, just to make sure there are no problems. Details.

Fernando, the evening maître d'hôtel, hurries in, late. A slight, bespectacled fellow, he cranes and spies constantly on the room. He is like some elegant, benign Edwardian mole from a children's book, always solicitous, constantly trying to polish the evening until it shines. A table which appears not to be having a positively perfect time is a continual reproach to him. If Mitch's job at lunch is to facilitate and smooth, Fernando's is to orchestrate. He conducts the long symphony of dinner with exacting delicacy, his great skill never to appear too busy. He can and does lean against the booking counter, his head resting on one hand, and talk about theatre or television, love affairs or traffic to anyone and everyone. His business is not so much food and service as harmony and melody. If everything goes right (and it usually does), the climax comes with a lot of violins and horns in the third and final movement. The after-theatre dinner is, above all, the Ivy's core business; this is what it does that no other restaurant in the City can do with such panache and drama.

Up the Paolozzi sculpted stairs, on the first floor, waiters are readying the private dining room for a dinner. It's an awkward space, bisected by a long pillar. There is a baby grand piano and the pictures are the grandparents of the ones downstairs. Modern British, from a time when men dressed in black tie to come to rooms like this. On the far side is a small service kitchen. The food is prepared two floors down in the main kitchen and finished here. The room is a popular place for book launches and celebratory meals and doesn't have that unloved, musty feel of most function rooms. Tonight an American pop star is being given dinner by her record company. They are imprecise about numbers and their PR is imperious. She's been here to recce the space and has rearranged it. Never mind that the Ivy does this three hundred days a year and is pretty clear on what works and what doesn't. She has organised parties for thousands and isn't taking advice from anyone. And there is some tricky placement to be navigated. A lot of big egos. The new table arrangement doesn't give the waiters enough room to get to all the guests, but they'll manage somehow. Out of the public eye, they banter as they flick the big tablecloths.

More worrying than the table plan is the menu. The record company has dismissed the Ivy's suggestions and insisted that the kitchen prepare a special dish, the singer's favourite pasta, with a sauce of unparalleled exquisite deliciousness that was invented especially for her by a very, very, very famous Italian chef. Mark Hix was entrusted with the recipe two days ago. His problem is that it doesn't work. He's made it five times: it's inedible. He's tried changing all the weights and measures: it still doesn't work. It's a worry. Either he calls the PR and admits he can't make it or he makes a well-known dish for which there are a dozen recipes of which this seems to be a variation.

5.30 P.M. The doorman is now in his top hat and green-faced livery. He opens the door for the first entrance of the evening, the first of up to seven hundred entrances and exits.

The first pre-theatre diners arrive. They tend to be slightly older than the later sittings, from a generation that doesn't mind eating when it's still light, and wouldn't sleep if they ate late. But there are young people here too. A family going to see a musical. Mother and father, brother and sister, the boy sullen in a new pair of long trousers and a sports jacket bought for growth. He's drawn the line at being parted from his trainers and shovels down one of the best hamburgers and fries in London.

'Better than McDonald's,' he grunts to his mother, who smiles at her husband and remembers the last time they were here, just the two of them. Too long.

The girl is just on the cusp of everything. More excited to be at the Ivy than she can contain. More embarrassed to be with her parents and brother than it's possible to bear.

This is a nice moment in the restaurant. The beginning of service. The customers expectant and happy, sloughing off the office frown, looking forward to the theatre. There is a smattering of first dates, blue-stocking girls with gleaming, sensibly cut hair and big handbags, boys with stripy suits and silly grins and nervous hands. On a banquette a white-haired, hand-knitted couple nod together over an ancient copy of Kobbe. The waiters shimmy swiftly across the room.

This is a very bad time to be in the kitchen. Evening service falls into three acts: pre-theatre, no theatre and post-theatre. Untheatrically, it starts with the climax. Theatre curtains go up at about seven thirty, and everyone has to be fed two, occasionally three, courses with enough time to get there and order the interval drinks. The head waiter can't hold up the orders now to ease the lot of the kitchen. They just have to get on with it.

The chef stands at the Pass, bellowing.

'Seventeen. Two Caesar, one Shepherd, one Fish of the Day, Pommes Allumettes. Table Twelve in one minute.'

The stations shout back.

'Chef.'

'Yes, chef.'

'Yes, chef.'

The kitchen gets through this hectic hour without a hitch only if the preparation is exact. In the quiet couple of hours between lunch and early dinner the cooks replenish the arsenal of partially prepared dishes, garnishes, chopped vegetables. Thousands of ingredients must be ready to hand during service because when the Remanco starts stuttering there will be no time to go off to duxelle mushrooms, mash potatoes or make crumble. One of the reasons that the Ivy is such a relaxed restaurant upstairs is because the preparation downstairs is so Germanic. All over the kitchen there are drawerfuls of pots, plastic trays, saucepans and buckets with all the deconstructed bits and pieces of dinner. Every surface and corner holds some essential piece of the massive mosaic of food that will make up the evening. Collectively the kitchen keeps a running reminder. It's the equivalent of twenty people simultaneously memorising the parts of fifty watches, every one of which they know will run out. Nothing has run out yet, but there is a shortage of silver chafing dishes.

'Dishes, dishes,' a sous-chef at the hob calls.

A kitchen porter slams cupboards, searches shelves.

Plating-up is an arcane craft that never crosses the mind of a normal mortal outside a commercial kitchen. Here it takes up a disproportionate amount of time and effort. You've had the same plates for years – that rather gaudy National Trust Wedgwood dinner service you got for a wedding present, the cheaper white ones bought for kids and kitchen suppers – and the serving dishes are a slow, alluvial sediment of earthenware, Pyrex, wood and stainless steel that's clunked and squatted in your kitchens from student digs to your first flat to your young-married quarters, and on and on all your life. Gimpy and dented, knobless and legless, the faithful retainers of a family. Nobody ever throws away kitchen equipment. You go through your clothes cupboard and your bathroom cabinet and the kids' toys with a puritan frenzy, but somehow throwing away the paraphernalia of sustenance would be like discarding old pets. The cutlery drawer becomes a retirement home for

Preceding pages: (left) *Memories of the Old Ivy*, Peter Blake (1990);
(right) *The Bathers*, Karl Hagedorn (1914–15)

unhinged salad tossers, bottle openers that have lost their grip and ridiculous, tiny coffee spoons from foreign hotels. When you dish up you just get a plate. When you need a serving dish you get the mashed potato, pasta and party salad one or the ovenproof bean and macaroni one.

It's not like that in a commercial kitchen. How a dish will go to the table is a matter of intense worry. Chefs talk about presentation more than you would ever imagine. Presentation is their public badge of office. Cooks serve food, chefs present food. In the Ivy there are dozens, hundreds of utensils to be remembered. Nothing just goes on a plate: it must all be as carefully dressed as a catwalk model. Ingredients may be added or dropped simply to suit a presentation. Not only must every dish on the menu be assembled in the same way every time, but it must fit into the broader scheme of things. Something like, say, a cassoulet wants to be offered in a bowl, but should it be served separately in a chafing dish because there are large, separate lumps of duck and sausage among the beans and the customer may prefer to arrange it personally? If you do that, though, an extra dish has to be carried by the runners and more space is taken up on the table - and the big bowl has to sit on the tray with a cloche on top and the other things stacked on top of that and the cloche on these particular dishes sits like last year's school cap.

Dishes, plates, glasses, salad plates, soy-sauce cups all have to be chosen not just for the rightness of their immediate task but to fit in with everybody else, and the twiddly little soy-sauce things are a particular bore because they keep going down the waste disposal.

And the chefs have a special fondness for silver tasting spoons. They keep them tucked in their belts like John Wayne's peacekeepers. Each has a particularly flash mannerism for the draw. Waiters squirrel away cutlery in their stations for an evening. Not being able to service a table fast because you run out of spoons because the chefs are playing Viva Zapata downstairs with their sauces is the sort of annoyance that frays tempers to shreds. There is a black market in certain items of crockery and silverware.

   The porter finds a stash of chafing dishes and the kitchen steams ahead. ➤156

Roasts, Grills and Entrées

Breast of Corn-Fed Chicken with Szechuan Vegetables

8 large corn-fed chicken breasts, trimmed of fat and sinew
vegetable oil for frying

For the Marinade
2 small red chillies, finely chopped
60 g fresh root ginger, finely chopped
10 g fresh coriander, finely chopped
40 ml sesame oil
40 ml vegetable oil
4 cloves garlic, peeled and finely chopped

For the Szechuan Vegetables
1 kg pak choi or any other Chinese greens,
   leaves removed and washed
80 ml sesame oil
60 g fresh root ginger, peeled and shredded
3 medium red chillies, seeded and shredded
2 cloves garlic, peeled and crushed
2 bunches spring onions, trimmed and shredded
   on the angle
400 g shiitake mushrooms (optional), quartered
15 g fresh coriander, roughly chopped
20 ml sweet soy or light soy sauce
salt and freshly ground black pepper

Place the chicken in a single layer in a dish. Mix together all the ingredients for the marinade, pour over the chicken and leave overnight.

Pre-heat the oven to 200°C/gas mark 6. Shake any excess marinade off the chicken breasts. Heat the vegetable oil in a pan and seal the chicken on both sides, then finish cooking them in the oven for 8–10 minutes.

Blanch the greens in boiling salted water for about 3 minutes until tender, drain and refresh them in cold water. Heat a wok, or a thick-bottomed cast-iron pan, and pour in the sesame oil. Fry the ginger, chillies, garlic and spring onions for 1–2 minutes (you may need to do this in two batches depending on the size of your pan). Add the Chinese greens, coriander and shiitake to the pan and sauté for a further 3-4 minutes. Finally add the soy sauce and remove the pan from the heat. Check the seasoning, then spoon the greens on to the middle of a large serving dish or on to individual plates, lay the chicken on top and spoon over some of the juices from the pan.

Chicken Masala

There has been confusion over this dish. Some people have ordered it and expected chicken in Marsala wine. Others cannot imagine what a curry is doing on the Ivy menu in the first place. But why shouldn't it be? Indian food is as much part of Britain's trade-borne culinary culture as French food. I call it empire food, not in a pejorative, colonising sense but to evoke an empire of food made unique to Britain by the sea.

salt and freshly ground black pepper
24 chicken thighs, boned and skinned
60 g clarified butter *or* ghee
1 tsp cumin seeds
2 tsp cumin powder
2 tsp turmeric
1 pinch saffron strands *or*
  $1/3$ tsp ground saffron
4 tsp curry powder
small piece cinnamon stick
good pinch curry leaves *or* 3 bay leaves
2 tsp paprika
4 cloves
1 tsp fenugreek seeds

1 tsp mustard seeds
3 medium onions, peeled and finely chopped
6 cloves garlic, peeled and crushed
85 g fresh root ginger, peeled and finely chopped
2 small chillies, finely chopped
200 g aubergine flesh, peeled and finely diced
2 tsp tomato purée
1 ltr Chicken Stock (see page 20)
$1/2$ lemon
100 g cream of coconut block
25 g coriander, chopped
8 servings Basmati Rice (see Kedgeree recipe
  on page 105)
70 g flaked almonds, lightly toasted

Season the chicken pieces. Heat the clarified butter in a large pan and fry the spices with the onions, garlic, ginger and chilli for a couple of minutes to release the flavours. Put in the chicken, the aubergine and the tomato purée, and cook for a further 5 minutes, stirring all the time.

Pour in the stock and add the lemon, then simmer gently for 45 minutes.

Check and correct the seasoning. The aubergines will have disintegrated by now and the sauce should be quite thick but, if not, simmer a little longer. If, on the other hand, the sauce has reduced too much, add some more stock or water.

Cut the cream of coconut into pieces, drop into the curry and stir until dissolved. Then put in the coriander and simmer for 5 minutes.

Serve the Chicken Masala accompanied by Basmati Rice with the almonds sprinkled over the top.

Oriental Pork Hot Pot

2 kg pork belly, boned, rind removed and cut into 8 cm x 4 cm chunks
plain flour, for dusting the pork
100 ml sesame oil
2 small onions, peeled and roughly chopped
2 medium mild red chillies, seeded and roughly chopped
200 g fresh root ginger, peeled and roughly chopped
4 star anise
8 cloves garlic, peeled and roughly chopped
2 tsp five-spice powder
100 ml light soy sauce
1 tsp fennel seeds
3 ltr Dark Meat Stock (see page 16)
30 g cornflour
salt and freshly ground black pepper

For the Garnish
3 large mild red chillies, seeded and cut into fine strips
80 g fresh root ginger, peeled and cut into fine strips
8 servings Chinese greens (see page 164)
2 bunches spring onions, trimmed and sliced on the angle
15 g coriander, washed

Lightly flour the pieces of pork belly. Heat some sesame oil in a thick-bottomed saucepan or flameproof casserole dish and quickly colour the pieces of pork on all sides.

Add the onions, chillies, ginger, star anise, garlic, five-spice, soy and fennel seeds. Pour over the meat stock, bring it to the boil, cover and simmer gently for $2^{1}/_{2}$–3 hours until the pork is very tender. If the liquid is evaporating too quickly, add some water.

Remove the pieces of pork from the pan. Mix the cornflour with a little water, stir it into the stock and simmer for 15 minutes – the consistency should be gravy-like. Check the seasoning and strain the sauce through a fine-meshed sieve. Return it to the pan with the pieces of meat.

Blanch the chillies and the ginger in boiling water for 4–5 minutes, refresh them in cold water and add them to the hot pot. Cook the Chinese greens as instructed on page 164 and arrange them on a serving dish or on individual plates. Spoon over the pieces of pork and a generous amount of sauce.

Stir fry the spring onions in the sesame oil and scatter them and the coriander leaves over the top of the hot pot.

Roast Partridge with Bread Sauce

The best partridge is the English grey-legged: it has a richer, more delicate flavour than the French or red-legged partridge, which is slightly bigger. Partridges must be eaten within a week of being shot and not hung too long or they become gamey and the delicate flavour is lost.

---

vegetable oil for deep-frying
3 large clean parsnips
200 ml Dark Meat Stock (see page 16)
200 ml Chicken Stock (see page 20)

salt and freshly ground black pepper
8 grey-legged English partridges, oven-ready
50 g butter
100 ml red wine

Pre-heat the oven to 240°C/gas mark 9. Heat some oil to 180°C in a deep-fat fryer. Top and tail the parsnips, leaving the skin on, unless it's very brown, and with a sharp mandolin (a slicing contraption with a very sharp blade – the Japanese ones are the best) slice them as thinly as possible lengthways, then dry them with a clean tea towel. Fry the slices in the hot fat a few at a time, stirring to ensure that they don't stick together. The parsnips will take a while to colour and may appear soft while they are still in the oil but once they have been drained they will dry out and crisp up. Leave them somewhere warm but not hot to dry.

Reduce together the dark meat and chicken stocks by two-thirds. Lightly season the partridges and rub the breasts with a little softened butter. Roast them in the oven for about 15 minutes. If you insert a sharp knife or carving fork between the legs and breast a little blood should run out. Slightly pink is the ideal way to serve partridge or they will be a little dry.

Leave the partridges on a plate to rest and to catch any juices that run out. Put the roasting tray in which they were cooked over a low heat, add the red wine and stir the bottom to remove any cooking residue. Reduce the red wine until almost evaporated and add the stock. Simmer until reduced by half, then strain the gravy through a fine-meshed sieve into a small pan. It should be thick enough now but, if not, mix a little cornflour with water and stir it in.

The partridges can be served whole or with the breasts and legs removed. Serve the Bread Sauce, parsnip chips and gravy separately or on the plate. Buttered Sprouts with Chestnuts (see page 160) would make an excellent accompaniment.

Bread Sauce

1 large onion, peeled and halved	1 ltr milk
100 g butter	salt and freshly ground black pepper
6 cloves	$\frac{1}{2}$ tsp ground nutmeg
1 bay leaf	200 g fresh white breadcrumbs

Finely chop one half of the onion and cook it gently in 50 g of the butter until soft. Stud the other half with the cloves, pushing them through the bay leaf to anchor it. Put the milk, nutmeg and studded onion into the pan with the cooked onion and bring it to the boil. Season, and simmer for 30 minutes. Remove the pan from the heat and leave the sauce to infuse for 30 minutes or so. Take out and discard the studded onion. Add the breadcrumbs and return the sauce to a low heat. Simmer for 15 minutes, giving it the occasional stir. Pour a third of the bread sauce from the pan into the blender and process, then return it to the pan and whisk in the remaining 50 g butter.

Escalope of Veal Holstein

8 x 150 g veal escalopes	75 ml vegetable oil for frying
salt and freshly ground black pepper	8 medium eggs
100 g plain flour	100 g butter
2 medium eggs, beaten	100 g capers, washed and drained
300 g white breadcrumbs	20 g parsley, washed and finely chopped
200 ml Dark Meat Stock (see page 16), reduced by two-thirds	16 anchovy fillets, cut in half lengthways

Season the escalopes, dip them first into the flour, then the beaten egg and last the breadcrumbs.

If necessary thicken the meat stock with a little cornflour mixed with water until it is of a thick, gravy-like consistency.

Heat the vegetable oil in a pan and fry the escalopes for 2–3 minutes on each side until they are golden. Keep them warm. Lightly fry the eggs and lay one on each veal escalope.

Melt the butter in a frying pan and cook it until it starts to turn a light brown. Add the capers and parsley and remove it from the heat. Spoon a little of the reduced meat stock on to a plate then lay the veal escalope and egg on top. Arrange 4 pieces of anchovy fillet on each egg and spoon over the caper and parsley butter.

Calves' Liver and Bacon

Good-quality calves' liver can be hard to find. If you have a good butcher, ask him to slice you some from a piece that's not too spongy, otherwise it can feel as if you are chewing cotton wool.

1 ltr Dark Meat Stock reduced by two-thirds (see page 16)	good-quality vegetable oil for frying
	250 g butter
24 rashers rindless streaky bacon, thinly sliced	10 g fresh sage
8 x 150 g slices calves' liver	8 servings Mashed Potato (see page 170)

Reduce the meat stock until it has thickened to a gravy-like consistency. If necessary, add a little cornflour mixed with some water. Crisp the bacon under a hot grill. Cook the liver, either by frying in oil or char-grilling it. Whichever way you choose, the pan or grill needs to be red-hot to seal the liver quickly and keep it pink. Melt the butter in a frying pan. When it is starting to brown, add the sage leaves and remove from the heat. Serve the liver on some mashed potato with the crisply grilled bacon and a little of the browned butter and sage, spooned over the top.

Confit of Duck

Order French duck legs, each weighing at least 300 g, from your butcher. Ask him to remove the thigh bone from the legs at the joint, leaving the flesh intact, and also to chop the end knuckle off each duck leg to expose the bone. Goose or duck fat can be bought in tins from a good butcher or delicatessen. Once the legs have been cooked in the fat, they can be left for up to a week until required and the fat frozen and used again.

8 large duck legs	80 g fresh root ginger, peeled
1 ltr Dark Meat Stock (see page 16)	2 bay leaves
75 ml red wine	10 g thyme
3 sticks cinnamon	12 cloves garlic, peeled and chopped
12 juniper berries, chopped	goose or duck fat
50 g coriander seeds	muslin and string
50 g white peppercorns	salt and freshly ground black pepper
25 g cloves	

Arrange the duck legs in a thick-bottomed pan, shaping them nicely so they present well when cooked. Cut a piece of muslin about 25 cm square, put all the herbs and spices into it, tie it with the string to make a bag and put it in with the duck legs. Melt the duck or goose fat and pour it over to cover them and season. Slowly bring the fat to the boil and simmer the legs gently for about 1½–2 hours. Test them by removing one: the meat should be very soft and tender and the leg still intact. Cool the legs and store them in the fat until required.

Preheat the oven to 230°C/gas mark 8. To serve the confit, remove the legs from the fat and roast them until they are crisp. This will take 30–40 minutes. Meanwhile, reduce the meat stock with the red wine by about two-thirds until it begins to thicken to a sauce-like consistency. If it doesn't thicken, stir in a little cornflour mixed with water. Serve the Confit with Mashed Neeps (see page 164) or Mashed Potato (see page 170) and the meat stock and red wine sauce. Alternatively, for a good summer salad, you could serve the hot, crisp duck on a frisé salad, dressed with vinaigrette (see page 49).

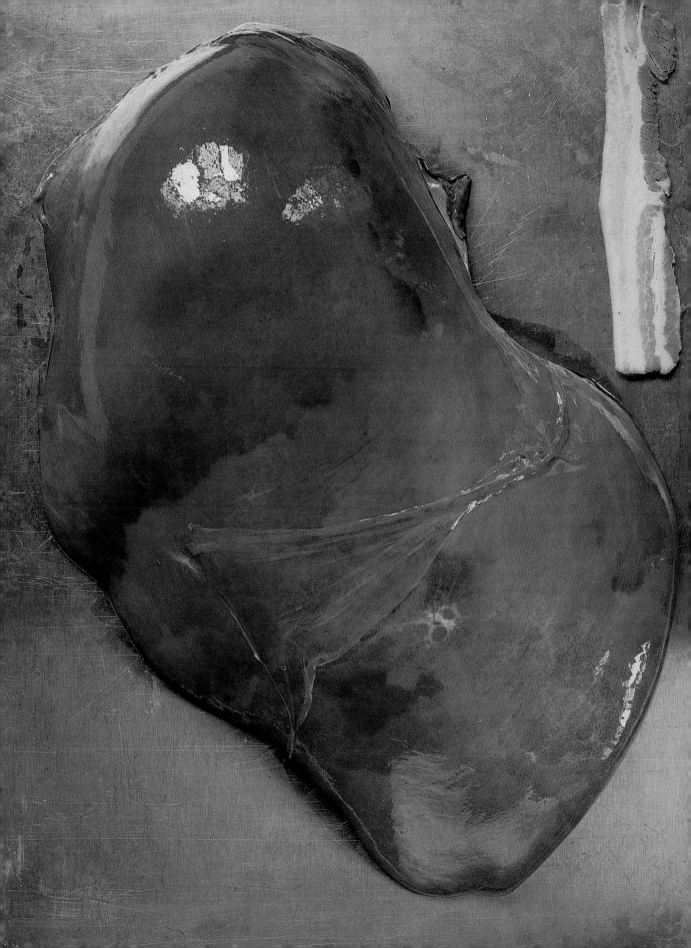

Steak Tartare

At the Ivy you can have this dish either ready-made or you can ask for an egg yolk to be served on the side for you to add to it yourself. If you're making it at home, I think the more you leave to your guests' individual taste the better. Some like it hot, some don't; some prefer it with onion, others without. Personally, I like to put in an anchovy. Whatever your preference, though, the one essential in this dish is the very best beef.

1 kg very fresh lean fillet,
  sirloin or topside steak, minced
1 medium red onion, peeled and finely chopped
140 g capers, drained and finely chopped
200 g shallots, peeled and finely chopped
15 ml brandy
2 tbsp tomato ketchup
2 tsp Worcestershire sauce
few dashes Tabasco sauce
3–4 tsp olive oil
salt and freshly ground black pepper

Ask your butcher to mince the meat through a clean mincer or, better still, do it yourself if you have a mincer attachment for your food processor.

Mix all the ingredients together and check the seasoning – you may wish to add a little more Tabasco, ketchup or Worcestershire sauce. Spoon the Steak Tartare on to a plate or, if you prefer, push it into a ramekin to mould it, then turn out on to a plate to serve. Serve with a Green Herb Salad (see page 80) and Pommes Allumettes (see page 170), or toast.

Roast Poulet des Landes

If I said I agreed to write this book primarily to learn how to make this dish it wouldn't be far from the truth. It is the main course that I eat most often at the Ivy. I dread the remote possibility that I might grow tired of it. Its main drawback is that you have to share it with someone and on the rare occasion that I've not been able to bully, cajole or flatter a companion into indulging me, I've just bought both halves and still thought it excellent value. The preparation looks complex but isn't. You can get the butcher to do the boning. At home we use those tins of foie gras pâté you can never remember buying but which seem to collect in larder corners like freemasons.

The Ivy uses chickens from Les Landes in south-west France but a good-quality free-range or corn-fed chicken will do the job. Fresh truffles and foie gras may be difficult to find but terrine or pâté de foie gras will be fine and a preserved truffle from a jar will give a good result. Serve accompanied by Buttered Sprouts with Chestnuts (see page 160) and Dauphin Potato (see page 170).

---

4 medium-size good quality chickens,
  minimum 1.2 kg each
50 g butter
10 medium shallots, peeled and finely chopped
300 g button mushrooms,
  washed and finely chopped
200 g fresh white breadcrumbs
200 g foie gras (fresh or pâté)

8 g parsley, finely chopped
salt and freshly ground black pepper
1 ltr Dark Meat Stock (see page 16)
500 ml Chicken Stock (see page 20)
1 black truffle, finely chopped
50 ml Madeira
Dauphin Potato (see page 170)

If you prefer, ask your butcher to prepare the legs for you. Otherwise, remove the legs from the chickens. Carefully, with the point of a sharp knife, cut around the thigh bone and half of the drumstick bone, keeping the flesh intact. Then chop through the drumstick bone with the heel of the knife. This will leave you with a two-thirds-boned chicken leg in one piece. Again with the heel of the knife, chop through the knuckle.

To make the stuffing, heat the butter in a pan and fry the shallots and mushrooms gently until they are soft. Mix in the breadcrumbs, then transfer it into a bowl. Dice the foie gras and add it to the stuffing with the chopped parsley, season, and mix well.

Put a good spoonful of stuffing into each leg and fold over the flesh to re-form the shape. Wrap each leg in cling-film a couple of times then cover in tin foil, ensuring that they are well sealed. Poach the legs in water for 10-12 minutes, then take them out and allow them to cool. Remove the foil and cling-film.

Reduce the dark meat and chicken stocks together by two-thirds until the liquid starts to thicken to a gravy-like consistency. Add the truffle to the stock with the Madeira. Reduce again to a gravy-like consistency.

Preheat the oven to 240°C/gas mark 9. Season the chicken breasts, and roast them on the bone for about 35-40 minutes. Put in the stuffed legs for the last 10-15 minutes, and baste them two or three times during cooking. Serve the breasts off the bone with the legs, the truffle sauce and dauphin potato.

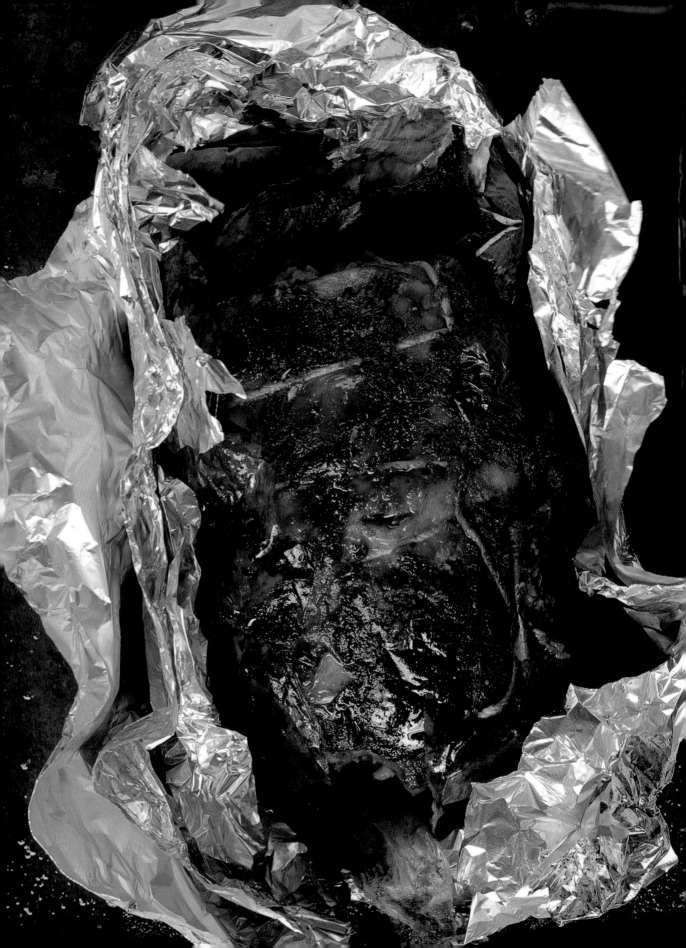

Slow-Baked Shoulder of Lamb

2 x 2-2.5 kg lamb shoulder, boned 1 ltr Dark Meat Stock (see page 16)	**For the Marinade** 10 cloves garlic, peeled and crushed 150 g fresh root ginger, peeled and crushed 3 medium chillies, finely chopped 3 tbsp ground cumin 75 ml olive oil salt and freshly ground black pepper grated zest of 2 lemons

Two days before you plan to serve the lamb, blend together the ingredients for the marinade and rub it into the lamb. Leave everything in a dish, covered with cling-film, in the fridge. Preheat the oven to 150°C/gas mark 2. Lightly season the lamb with salt, wrap it in foil and bake for 4–4½ hours. Remove the lamb from the foil and place it on a serving dish. Strain the juices into a saucepan and add the dark meat stock. Reduce the mixture by half, or until it thickens, then strain it through a fine-meshed sieve. Slice the meat and serve with the sauce separate. Some warmed Chick-pea Relish (see page 52) makes an excellent accompaniment to the lamb.

Shepherd's Pie

900 g each good quality minced
  lamb and beef, mixed and not too fatty
vegetable oil for frying
500 g onions, peeled and finely chopped
2 cloves garlic, peeled and crushed
10 g thyme, chopped finely
	25 g flour
	2 tbsp tomato purée
	150 ml red wine
	50 ml Worcestershire sauce
	1 ltr Dark Meat Stock (see page 16)
	8 half servings of firm Mashed Potato,
	  with no cream added (see page 170)
	salt and freshly ground black pepper

Season the minced meat. Heat some vegetable oil in a frying pan until it is very hot and cook the meat in small quantities for a few minutes, then drain it in a colander to remove all the fat. In a thick-bottomed pan, heat some more vegetable oil and gently fry the onion, garlic and thyme until they are very soft. Add the meat, dust it with flour and add the tomato purée. Cook for a few minutes, stirring constantly.

Preheat the oven to 200°C/gas mark 6. Slowly add the red wine, Worcestershire sauce and dark meat stock, bring it to the boil and simmer for 30–40 minutes. Strain off about 200 ml of the sauce to serve with the pie. Continue to simmer the meat until the liquid has almost evaporated. Take it off the heat, check the seasoning and allow it to cool. To make the pie, put the meat into a large serving dish or individual dishes and top with potato. Bake for 35–40 minutes. A good accompaniment for Shepherd's Pie is Mashed Neeps (see page 164).

The Ivy Hamburger

This is what Jeremy calls an 'attitude dish'. Even if you don't eat it, seeing it on the menu tells you that this isn't a stuffy restaurant that's going to make you eat three courses, all with pretentious sauces. You should order it. It's the best classic hamburger to be had in London. If you pick it up, they'll give you a finger bowl. Jeremy has a particular 'Well, blow me' look when Americans tell him that it's better than they get at home.

1.4 kg good quality minced beef, including 20–30 per cent fat	2 medium red onions, peeled and thinly sliced into rings
80 g American mustard	8 large sweet pickled gherkins, sliced
320 g tomato ketchup	2 beef tomatoes, sliced
8 good quality baps	salt and freshly ground black pepper

Mix the mince to ensure that the fat is evenly distributed throughout, then mould into 8 balls and shape with a burger press, if you possess one, or by pushing the meat into a pastry cutter. Then put the hamburgers into the fridge to set the meat before cooking. Whisk together the tomato ketchup and American mustard for the hamburger sauce.

Lightly toast the baps and keep them warm until you have cooked the burgers. The hamburgers are best cooked on a hot barbecue or griddle plate but a smoking hot cast-iron pan will do: this seals in the juices and will give a nicely cooked rare or medium-rare burger in a couple of minutes without the juices running out. Don't cook them under the grill unless you have a red-hot American-style one, as this tends to boil the meat and it becomes dry and lacks flavour.

Serve the hamburgers in the baps with slices of red onion, gherkin, beef tomato and the hamburger sauce.

Overleaf: Shepherd's Pie

6.30 P.M. Outside it's a damp, chilly evening. A shower has left the streets slick and varnished. The Ivy's blue-moon, stained-glass window shimmers in the gutter like a little literary pun on George Orwell's impossibly perfect hostelry, the Moon in a Puddle. Opposite, The Mousetrap, lit up and boastful as the longest-running play in the world, prepares for its umpteenth performance before yet another crowd of bussed-in vacuum-cleaner assemblers from the Midlands and a smattering of spectacularly unadventurous Americans ready to be astounded that the murderer is... No, it isn't in the spirit of the Ivy to spoil even a tired theatrical moment. But when Richard Attenborough took his first bow after the first performance the Ivy was already an old trouper. These two dowagers of 'Theatreland', as the street signs wince-makingly put it, bask in each other's reflected neon.

The Ivy is at the oblique corner of two streets, a quiet, difficult-to-arrive-at junction between the congestion of Litchfield Street to the south and West Street to the north. In the doorway stands the doorman, rubbing his gloved hand, like a gun in a butt awaiting the first covey. He is a jolly man, a personable 'Hail fellow, well met' chap. A man who knows to a nicety what the customer expects from Central Casting by way of a doorman. He stands wrapped in his Mr Bumble uniform of great coat and top hat with green facings, a scarf neatly tucked into his lapel. The only tell-tale sign that this top-of-the-morning Irishman might not be quite as stereotypical as he seems is the very chic, bright Richard James chequered silk tie. A doorman's job is all about appearances, about performance. The audience sees the doorman for a brief moment only, but he has to leave an impression. He is an exemplar of Stanislavsky's dictum that there are no small parts, just small actors. This grinning, amiable chap, with an encyclopædic memory for faces and names, packs into his walk-on all the show-stopping blarney of one of A Midsummer's Night's Dream's rude mechanicals. Actually, of course, it's you that walks on while he stays put, repeating the same moves and dialogue for each member of his audience.

The doorman, like the hat-check on the other side of this door, is of the restaurant but not exactly part of its inner workings. His fiefdom is the street, cars and taxis, and jolly efficient he is at it too. A bit of a miracle worker. When London's clogged to stasis, when there isn't a yellow light on a black cab between here and Wimbledon, the doorman will have something up his sleeve or hidden round the corner, and, inside, the managers have more sense than to enquire quite how he manages to be so efficient. He is the Ivy's Sergeant Bilko. It's a worldwide tradition that doormen know the angles, exploit the wrinkles. Gents of the world also know, or think they know, that the short cut to better service is to see the doorman 'all right'.

The doorman's other job is to protect customers from the paparazzi. There are always one or two standing in the alley opposite, opportunists looking for a third page in the early edition of the Standard or, perhaps, that one flashed moment catching the escaped nipple or the knickerless exit from a limo. Perhaps even the cannily provoked punch that will wire round the world and make a holiday home in Cannes or a new, top-of-the-range BMW.

The Ivy has an uneasy relationship with these photographers. By nature Jeremy, Chris and the restaurant are discreet and private. No one has ever photographed inside. They never give interviews and they will never confirm or deny that anyone has dined here. But publicity is at the heart of many of their customers' businesses and fame isn't hurt by photographers, so, while some mind and some court while pretending to mind, well, the paparazzi are a grey area. Every so often Jeremy puts his foot down and threatens to ban a too-insistent photographer - this can be done by threatening the status quo with the others. A powerful halogen torch is kept in the office. If it's shone at the pack, their negatives will look like Antarctica in a snowstorm.

Preceding page: The Ivy Hamburger

'I've only had to hit one once,' says the doorman, 'when a film star was getting into her car. They surged. It was frightening.'

On the opposite corner, slightly apart from the photographers, is a small group. Rubberneckers. Amateur star snappers with cheap Instamatics and cans of soda. They are a sorry bunch who come here in a van from Liverpool, presumably because if you're going to hang around on a street corner it might as well be a glamorous one. Better a view of the Ivy than some northwestern chippie. But still, the presence of these middle-aged lads kicking the walls of the theatre and their time-wasting chat are an uncomfortable counterpoint to the purposeful, project-rich crowd inside. They are separated by more than a road. There is no moral to be gleaned from this, no urban social truths; just the observation that cities are ever thus. The Ivy is a special place because a lot of the rest of the city isn't.

Around the side of the restaurant's liner-like prow the glass cobbles shine with the light of the kitchens. Open iron vents waft the smell and noise of the steamy heat into the humming quiet of the street.

The doorman rubs his palms and stamps. ➤172

Vegetables

Bubble and Squeak

Bubble and squeak is traditionally made from leftover vegetables and potatoes. This version uses fresh, but frying the mixture twice gives it an authentic flavour.

400 g swede, peeled and cut into chunks
good vegetable oil for frying
5 medium onions, peeled and sliced
400 g green cabbage, sliced, *and/or* Brussels sprouts, outer leaves removed
salt and freshly ground black pepper
350 g firm Mashed Potato, no butter or cream added (see page 170)
plain flour for dusting

Bring a saucepan of salted water to the boil, put in the swede and cook until soft. Heat 3 tbsp vegetable oil in a pan and cook the sliced onions until they are soft. Cook the cabbage until soft in boiling salted water. Cook the sprouts until soft, then slice them. Put all the cooked vegetables together in a bowl, mix well and season.

Heat some more vegetable oil in a non-stick or heavy-bottomed frying pan until it is almost smoking and fry the mixture a little at a time until it colours, turning with a wooden spoon. Then return to the bowl and leave it to cool. Mix in the mashed potato, check the seasoning, then mould the bubble and squeak into even-sized cakes. Refrigerate them overnight. When you are ready to serve them, lightly flour the cakes and heat some vegetable oil in a frying pan. Cook them on both sides until they are golden brown.

Buttered Sprouts with Chestnuts

Chestnuts can now be bought in vacuum tins or bags, ready peeled and cooked – much more convenient than having to do the job yourself.

1 kg small Brussels sprouts, outer leaves removed
250-300 g ready-peeled vacuum-packed chestnuts *or* 1 kg fresh chestnuts, roasted and peeled
100 g butter
salt and freshly ground black pepper

Bring a pan of salted water to the boil and cook the sprouts for 8-10 minutes. Meanwhile, roast the chestnuts in a little of the butter in the oven or under the grill. Drain the sprouts and toss with the chestnuts in the remaining butter. Season to taste.

Deep-Fried Hash Browns

30 g butter
2 medium onions, peeled and thinly sliced
1 kg large potatoes, cooked in their skins, peeled and grated
1 medium egg white, half beaten
200 g dry Mashed Potato, no cream or butter added (see page 170)
50 g potato flour
1/2 tsp celery salt
salt and freshly ground black pepper
good vegetable oil for deep-frying

Heat the butter in a pan and cook the onions slowly until they are soft. Put the onions into a bowl, add the grated potato and mix them together with the egg white. Stir in the mashed potato, the potato flour, celery salt and seasoning. If the mixture is a little wet, add some more potato flour.

Preheat a deep-fat fryer to 170°C with 8 cm oil. Test the mixture by rolling a couple of little balls of it in the palm of your hand and dropping them into the hot fat. When they are cooked, taste them and, if necessary, adjust the seasoning. Then roll the rest into walnut-sized balls and cook them in batches.

Note: You can half fry the Hash Browns in advance, then crisp them up in hot oil before you serve them.

Gratin of Butternut Squash

1.5 kg butternut squash, peeled, halved, seeds removed and sliced thinly
700 ml double cream
10g thyme, leaves removed and chopped
6 cloves garlic, peeled and crushed
120 g freshly grated Parmesan cheese
salt and freshly ground black pepper

Pre-heat the oven to 175°C/gas mark 4. Put the squash slices into a bowl. Take a saucepan and bring the cream, thyme, garlic and half of the Parmesan to the boil, season and remove it from the heat. Mix half of the cream mixture with the sliced squash, then lay the slices in an ovenproof serving dish 5-6 cm deep. Pour all of the remaining cream mixture over the squash, then sprinkle with the remaining Parmesan. Sit the dish in a larger one, a third filled with hot water, as a bain marie – a deep-sided roasting tin would be good. Bake in the oven for about 1 hour until nicely browned, or finish the dish by glazing it under the grill.

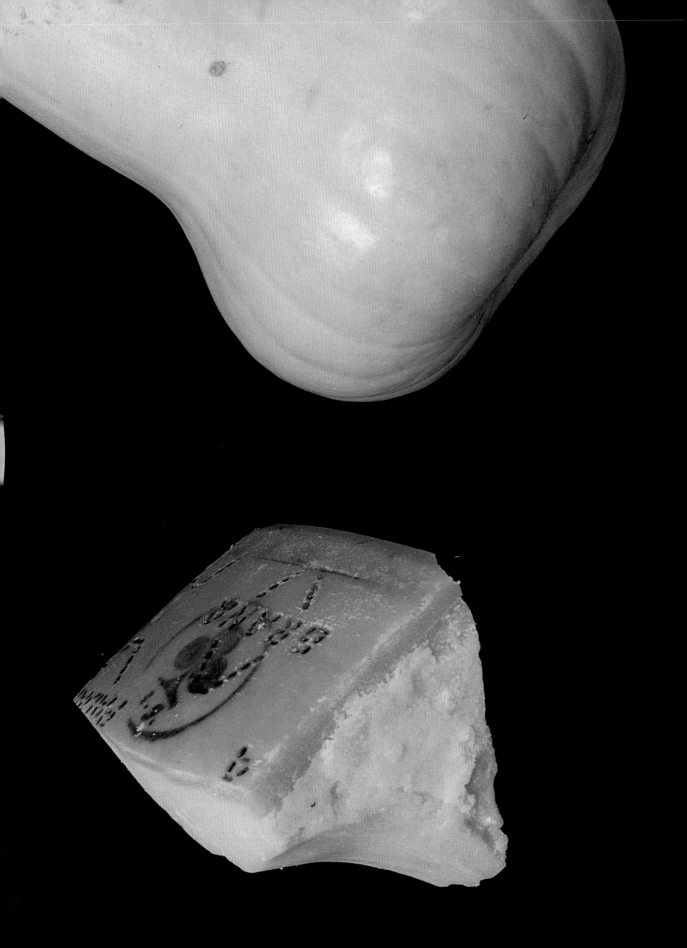

Mashed Neeps

Mashed, or Bashed, Neeps are traditionally made with swede, cooked in boiling salted water then mashed, although a good alternative is to use half swede and half parsnip. Mix in a generous amount of butter, according to taste, salt and freshly ground black pepper. Allow about 200 g per person.

Parmesan-Fried Courgettes with Pesto

8 medium courgettes	**For the Pesto**
2 medium eggs	80 g basil
50 ml milk	2 cloves garlic, peeled and crushed
4 tbsp plain flour, seasoned	30 g pine nuts, lightly roasted
salt and freshly ground black pepper	150 ml extra-virgin olive oil
100 g Parmesan, grated	50 g Parmesan, grated
good vegetable oil for deep-frying	

To make the pesto, put all the ingredients in a blender and process until smooth. Cut the courgettes into three, crossways, then each third into eight. Have ready four dishes. Place the flour in the first. In the second, beat together the eggs and the milk. Place the grated Parmesan in the third. The fourth will hold the prepared courgettes. Coat the courgette pieces with the flour, then the egg, and last the Parmesan. Make sure that you shake off any excess flour before dipping them in the egg or the Parmesan will not stick. Heat a deep-fat fryer to 160–170°C with 10 cm of vegetable oil and cook the courgettes until they are golden. Drain them on kitchen paper and season lightly. Serve them with a little pesto spooned on top

Stir-Fried Chinese Greens

1 kg pak choi or any other Chinese greens, washed and sliced	3 medium, mild red chillies, seeded and shredded
80 ml sesame oil	2 bunches spring onions, trimmed and sliced on the angle
4 cloves garlic, peeled and crushed	30 g fresh coriander, roughly chopped
160 g fresh root ginger, peeled and sliced	20 ml soy sauce
	salt and freshly ground black pepper

Blanch the greens for 3-4 minutes in boiling, salted water, then refresh them in cold water and drain. Heat the sesame oil in a wok or thick-bottomed pan. Fry the garlic, ginger and chilli for a few seconds then add the spring onions and greens. Cook on a high heat for 2–3 minutes. Add the coriander to the greens, pour in the soy, toss, check the seasoning and serve immediately.

Honey-Roasted Parsnips

1.5 kg young parsnips	3 tbsp clear honey
100 g beef dripping	salt and freshly ground black pepper

If the skins of the parsnips are clean they need not be peeled. Otherwise, top and tail, peel and quarter them lengthways. Remove the hard core that runs down the centre and can be a little woody.

Preheat the oven to 200°C/gas mark 6. Blanch the parsnips in boiling, salted water for 5-6 minutes and drain them. Heat a roasting tray in the oven with the beef dripping and add the parsnips. Season, and roast them for about 30 minutes, turning occasionally until they are nicely coloured. Add the honey, turn the parsnips and return the tray to the oven, basting with the honey and dripping until they are golden. Serve immediately.

Roasted Vine Tomatoes with Chilli Salsa

Vine tomatoes have been ripened and sold on the vine rather than having been picked and sent to the store in a box. Just because they are on the vine, though, does not necessarily mean they taste good, so check them out first. This dish makes a good starter or accompaniment to a main course. Always check the strength of the chillies before using them.

200 ml extra-virgin olive oil	8 small shallots or 1 medium onion, peeled and
2 large red peppers,	finely chopped
seeded and finely chopped	30 ml balsamic vinegar
2-3 medium-sized red and green chillies,	15 g fresh coriander, washed and finely chopped
seeded and finely chopped	16–24 tomatoes on the vine (allow 2-3 tomatoes
salt and freshly ground black pepper	per person, depending on their size)

Heat half of the olive oil in a pan and cook the peppers and chillies slowly with the shallots, stirring constantly for 2–3 minutes. Add the balsamic vinegar, coriander and another 50 ml of the olive oil, season a little, remove from the heat and leave the Chilli Salsa to stand for an hour or so.

Preheat the oven to 200°C/gas mark 6. Bring a large pan of water to the boil and have some iced water nearby. Cut the tomato stems so that two or three are linked together for each portion. Plunge the tomatoes a few at time into the boiling water for 10–12 seconds then plunge them into the cold water. The skins should now peel easily but, if not, plunge them back into the boiling water for a few more seconds.

Dry the tomatoes on some kitchen paper. Pour the remaining olive oil into an oven tray and heat it in the oven. Season the tomatoes and roast them, basting them with the oil from time to time, until they are lightly coloured. Serve with a couple of spoons of Chilli Salsa.

Potatoes

Many restaurants now use frozen chips, but they are never as good as the real thing. The Ivy encounters all sorts of problems in trying to find the correct potato to use for chips: during storage the starch in potatoes turns to sugar and chips don't become crisp when they are fried. Also, you need large potatoes to make the long Pommes Allumettes and big potatoes don't always make good chips. However, a good baking potato, such as Desirée or Maris Piper, will usually provide decent ones.

Chips and Allumettes

There are all sorts of different chip cutters these days, so if you want Allumettes, fine cut, or chips, thick cut, use the appropriate attachment or gadget. Alternatively, you can, of course, simply use a good sharp knife.

Allow 225–250 g of potatoes per person. Peel and square off the ends. For thick-cut chips cut each potato into 1 cm slices then cut the slices into 1 cm wide chips. Do the same for allumettes but cut them to $^1/_2$ cm wide. Wash the chips or allumettes, then drain them on kitchen paper.

Preheat 12 cm of vegetable oil to 120°C in a deep-fat fryer. Blanch the chips two or three handfuls at a time until they are soft but not coloured. Remove them from the fat and drain. You can store the chips in this state in the fridge for a couple of days. To serve the chips, re-fry them in hot fat (160–180°C) until they are crisp, season them lightly with salt and serve them immediately.

Mashed Potato

As a rule, potatoes that chip well mash well. King Edwards are also good for mashing. Peel and cut the potatoes into even-sized pieces. Cook them in boiling, salted water, drain them and then return them to the pan over the heat to remove any excess moisture. Using an old-fashioned masher, a food processor or a potato ricer, purée them and mix them with plenty of good butter, a little double cream, and check the seasoning.

Dauphin Potato

1.5 kg medium-sized potatoes, peeled and thinly sliced
50 ml extra virgin olive oil
salt and freshly ground black pepper

Preheat the oven to 200°C/gas mark 6. Heat two 20 cm cast iron frying pans (or one 26 cm) on top of the stove or in the oven. Remove them from the heat, then rub the bottom of the pan with a little oil and lay the potatoes around it covering the surface (the bottom becomes the top in the finished dish). Continue to lay the potatoes in, lightly seasoning every couple of layers and rubbing the potatoes with a little more oil until they are all in the pans. Then bake in the oven for 1 hour. If the potatoes are beginning to turn brown on top, cover them with foil. Test that they are cooked with the point of a knife in the centre. Turn the potato cakes out onto a chopping board and cut them into equal wedges.

8.30 P.M. The restaurant is full. Eight thirty is the most popular time for dinner in Britain. By some sort of national osmosis we've decided that this is the ideal time to eat. If we were in France we would be thinking about where to go; in Spain we'd still be in our socks and underpants watching the beginning of a movie on television, confident that we'd be able to see the end before dinner time. If we were in the American Midwest we'd just be finishing our decaffeinated herbal tea and calling for the bill. But here eight thirty is when convention, digestion and baby-sitters say we should eat.

The bar is filling up. It might just be my luck, but there always seem to be a lot of modishly cropped young men in the bar. Today they are sitting at the round table with one girl with gypsy eyes and Paloma Picasso lips. She might be Carmen tearing the tips off her cigarettes. Her attendant toreadors – four designers from the ballet and St Martin's – drink beer and wave their hands. In a corner are three girls, huge bosoms cantilevered precipitously into black frocks. They are laughing and the bosoms rock together and apart across their round table like those little pecking chicken toys from Prague.

Restaurant bars are usually problem areas, a waiting room pretending to be a bar. A place where the mistakes and the wishful thinking of the reservations book have to kick their heels over a complimentary glass of sour bubbly. Where young men face the growing realisation that they've been stood up. But not the Ivy's. The bar here has its own microclimate, jolly, filled with expectation and banter. Often, I've seen a manager come to a group and tell them that their table is ready, only to be greeted with a look of mild annoyance.

'We'll be there in a minute.'

The barman's job is one of the most demanding in the restaurant. Not only must he supply the drinks, salted almonds and the Ivy's famous garlicky olives, but he also has to take the food orders from the little tables here. There can be up to thirty people milling about at once. The thing that makes this bar so gemütlich is that so many of the customers know each other. Chances are that someone walking in for dinner will be on first-name terms with someone drinking. In fact you're more likely to be on first-name terms with people at the Ivy than on surname terms. It's not that the London arts world is small or tight-knit – it's actually rather large – but everyone in it tends to know a lot of people vaguely, a bit. The web of networking is essential for those who are freelance, who never know when or with whom they'll work. The arts community is a loose, peripatetic herd that circles from job to project to sabbatical. And then, of course, there is the freemasonry of fame, or near fame, or potential fame. There is a television presenter whom I see here quite frequently at lunch, though we've never been introduced. As far as I know this is the only room I've ever been in with him, but every time he waves or pats me on the back and says, 'Hi.' I'm not even sure he doesn't think I'm that bloke on breakfast TV.

In the restaurant at least eight people are on their feet talking, glad-handing, with fellows at other tables. Not talking business, not saying much – only what advertising men call brand-recognition, just saying, 'I'm still here. Next time you think you might need someone in my line you'll remember me, won't you?' or 'I might remember your girlfriend topless when I'm filling up the house in Tuscany.' This table-hopping business, so easily derided, is an essential part of the arts and media world. You couldn't begin to count the number of magazine features, films, television programmes, theatre productions, books, radio series that have their genesis or some part of their history in this room. To the terminally cynical it might look like a lot of luvvies air-kissing, but it's the laboratory that produces a good deal of the stuff you call culture, the essential pleasures of modern existence. You can't divorce these small, arch meetings from the book that changed your life, the film that made you cry or the slow ballad that is forever your and her love song. It was really rather a stroke of genius by the arts community to have arranged their market over lunch in this dining room rather than on some sweaty dealing floor or in a clingfilm sandwich-stacked boardroom.

A steady stream of theatricals pause at the corner table where a few hours ago the weekly tasting meeting was held. A rheumy-eyed old man and a small, elegantly ancient woman sit smiling and nodding and eating tiny neat forkfuls. His face would be recognised in any country that has electricity. It has been for more than a generation. The theatrical knight. The man who was a star before Pinter, before Osborne, who knew Rattigan when he was in amateur dramatics at university, whose Shakespeare performances are still definitive, the star of a fistful of classic films, a man who has an Oscar in black and white. He has known everyone in the movies and theatre for a lifetime, but they're all dead now and he knows almost no one. But everyone knows him, and they come to nod and smile shyly and mumble plaudits which his discreet hearing aid can't pick up over the clatter of cutlery. They come because in forty years' time they want to be able to sit where he's sitting and say to people much like themselves: 'Oh, yes, I remember him. Sir Rowland. Wonderful old chap. Of course, he was getting along a bit - aren't we all?'

The theatrical knight looks out over the room and considers his status as a national treasure. His joints feel as if they're already fifty per cent memorial. The room is full of ghosts, of stiff tulle dresses and gardenias on the shoulder, full of dinner jackets and the smell of brilliantine mixed with gin. Nobody drinks cocktails any more, do they? This room is more precious to him than any other. It's a stage where his friends still live, as echoes to the contemporary laughter.

9.30 P.M. Chris arrives from Le Caprice and glances at the reservations book. The maître d'hôtel of the evening has a quite different job from his lunch-time equivalent. Whereas lunch might be Terence Rattigan, dinner is Cecil B. de Mille. Fernando manages the extras, building the atmosphere to maximum effect. Chris has a word with the manager and looks over the restaurant like a pointer that's just been let out of a Land-Rover into a very promising field of stubble. He sniffs the air, tastes the atmosphere, picks up the detail - the uneasy customer, a delayed dessert, someone trying to attract another bottle of claret. There's a quivering thirty seconds while he absorbs the room. Good. It's good tonight. The buzz, the feeling of enjoyment, expectation, it's jelling. The mix is right, the right balance of pretty and witty. Enough listeners for the garrulous, no tables of dumbly bored couples emanating gloom. The laughter is well orchestrated and scattered around the room. There is a pretty face and a famous face in everyone's eyeline. The most complicated soufflé in catering has risen. He starts his tour of the tables. He has a less magisterial presence than Jeremy, he flits rather than parades; characteristically, he bends towards customers in an intimate moment. He remembers everything, last performances, best books. He reads, or sounds as if he's read, everything everyone in the room has ever said or written. All the time he is talking and smiling across the room he has an eye on the staff, noticing the gravy stain on the apron, the forgotten spoon. This casual walkabout can take up to an hour, but the concentration never falters. The restaurant is at full speed. One wrong move, one mistake, one glass too many and the carapace of enthusiasm can be punctured, the atmosphere escape and the whole room collapse.

There is a sound of slithering. Unremarkable to the untrained ear, it's followed immediately by a loud crash.

10.00 PM 'Fuck, fuck, fuck.' A runner has dropped a tray, a whole tray. Dinner for a table of four has fed gravity. Two Cassoulet, Sea Bass, chips, Caesar Salad, plates, tin cloches, the whole sodding lot on the floor. Missed the bloke by that much. The runner is going to brazen it out. He stands at the Pass like a footballer who's been shown the red card for a professional foul.

'The first time in three years; the first time in three years.'

He repeats it in case the hors d'oeuvres didn't quite hear. No one's blaming him. The chef isn't shouting. It's amazing that it doesn't happen more often, and he's good. He's a good runner. It's just a bloody nuisance, though. The flow of food has to be stopped so that the order can be repeated ahead of the line. Everything has been going so smoothly, the kitchen has been working with the rhythm of a galley. It's no accident that the word for a ship's kitchen and the benches where slaves rowed is the same.

'It could have been worse,' another runner says, happy it wasn't him.
'It could have been worse – it could have been on the stairs.'
'I've never done that – oh, quick, touch wood.'
'It's those cassoulet plates,' he adds, 'the cloches don't fit exactly.'
Yes, that must be it.
'Funny, though, I felt it going. Felt the weight shifting, nothing I could do. Missed him by this much.'
The floor of the kitchen is treacherous, a slick film covering everything. A porter pushes a long mop like an ancient Rastafarian's head round the walkways.

'Special. Table Fifteen. One minute.'
'Yes, chef.'
'Yes, chef.'
The dinner comes again. The runner puts it carefully on the tray, arranging the cloches. It's like falling off a horse - you've got to get right back on. He hoists the tray and slithers towards the stairs like an overloaded seaplane. The kitchen listens.➤200

Preceding page: (above) *The Professionals*, Tom Phillips (1990); (below) *The Actor*, Eduardo Paolozzi (1984)

Desserts, Puddings and Savouries

Chocolate or Vanilla Sponge **180** Chocolate Pudding Soufflé **180** Baked Alaska **181**
Bramley Apple Crumble with Devonshire Clotted Cream **184** Cappuccino Brûlé **186**
Caramelised Bread and Butter Pudding **188** Rice Pudding with Armagnac Prunes **188**
Cinnamon Roasted Fruits with Mascarpone **189** Gooseberry and Elderflower Fool **189**
Scandinavian Iced Berries with Hot White Chocolate Sauce **190**
Mousse aux deux Chocolats **192** Amaretto Chocolate Truffles **192** Tiramisu **193**
Sticky Toffee Pudding **194**

Welsh Rarebit **196** Reggiano Parmesan with Pickled Plum Tomatoes **196**
Farmhouse Cheddar with Crumpets and Onion Chutney **197** Herring Roes on Toast **198**
Scotch Woodcock **198**

Chocolate or Vanilla Sponge

Makes 2 x 25 cm sponges. You can use the same recipe for both the chocolate and vanilla sponges: replace 30 g of the flour with 30 g of cocoa powder for the chocolate cake.

3 medium eggs	a few drops vanilla essence
150 g caster sugar	(vanilla sponge only)
	150 g plain flour, sieved

Pre-heat the oven to 220°C/gas mark 7. Lightly butter and dust with flour the insides of two 25-cm sandwich tins or one deep tray. In a clean mixing bowl, using an electric whisk, or in a food processor or mixer at a high speed, whisk together the eggs and sugar until they are the consistency of thick cream and doubled in volume. Add the vanilla essence if you are making a vanilla sponge. Remove the mixture from the machine and, with a large spoon, gently fold in the flour. Carefully transfer the mixture into the prepared tins or tray and bake for 25-30 minutes. Test whether the sponge is cooked by pressing the centre with your finger: it should be firm to the touch. Turn out on to a cooling wire or cake rack and leave to cool.

Chocolate Pudding Soufflé

Griotte cherries are a luxury option in this recipe if you can find them. Use them, if possible, as they give a nice alcoholic kick to the pudding.

butter for greasing	4 egg yolks
a little caster sugar for dusting	65 g caster sugar
$1/2$ Chocolate Sponge recipe baked in	55 g strong plain flour, sifted
a tray (see above)	100 g jar Griottines or Morello cherries
530 g good quality dark chocolate or buttons	in syrup or alcohol
210 g butter	a little icing sugar for dusting
5 g fresh yeast (or equivalent amount of dried yeast)	250 g crème fraîche
2 medium eggs	

Lightly butter and dust with caster sugar the inside of 8 x 8 cm stainless-steel rings, or deep egg rings. Cut 8 discs of sponge $1/2$ cm thick and place them inside the rings on a baking sheet 7.5 cm apart. Melt the chocolate and butter in a bowl over a pan of simmering water and bring to blood temperature, stirring constantly, ensuring that no water spills into the chocolate. Put in the yeast and stir until it has dissolved, then remove the pan from the heat and pour the mixture into a bowl.

Preheat the oven to 190°C/gas mark 5. In a food processor or mixer, whisk the eggs, egg yolks and sugar together on a high speed until the mixture has doubled in volume. Pour this slowly into the chocolate and mix carefully. Fold in the flour. Divide the mixture between the 8 rings, filling them 1 cm from the top, place 5 Griottines into the top of each soufflé and bake for 9–10 minutes. When they are cooked, the soufflés should still be soft in the centre. Remove them from the rings, with the help of a small sharp knife, and dust with a little icing sugar. Serve with crème fraîche, a few more Griottines and a little of the preserving liquid from the jar.

Baked Alaska

If everything is made fresh, Baked Alaska is an all-day job, so buy good-quality sorbet, ice cream and a sponge, or make one in advance. The flavours of the sorbet and ice cream can be varied to give a seasonal touch.

---

500 ml vanilla ice cream
500 ml raspberry sorbet
350 g caster sugar

150 ml eau-de-vie de framboise
1 Vanilla Sponge Cake (see page 180)
4 medium egg whites

Remove the ice cream and sorbet from the freezer about 10 minutes before you assemble the Alaska.

Bring 100 ml water and 100 g of the caster sugar to the boil, cool a little and add 100 ml of the eau-de-vie de framboise.

Cut the sponge into three discs 7–8 mm thick. Put one layer on to an ovenproof serving dish and brush it generously with the sugar syrup. Spread the ice cream over the sponge, leaving 2 cm of sponge at the edge. Spread the sorbet over the middle of the ice cream leaving 2 cm of ice cream at the edge. Put it into the freezer until it is firm.

Cut the two remaining discs of sponge in half, then cut three of the halves in half again. Cut the remaining half into a circle with a 10-cm cutter if you have one, otherwise use a sharp knife.

Remove the Alaska from the freezer and place the disc of sponge in the middle of the sorbet. Use the quarter pieces to cover the rest of the sorbet and ice cream, overlapping the disc in the middle and meeting the piece of base sponge. This protects the sorbet and ice cream from melting when it is baked. Brush the top of the sponge generously with the sugar syrup and return it to the freezer.

To make the meringue, bring 100 ml water and the rest of the caster sugar (250g) to the boil, stirring occasionally. Continue boiling until the syrup starts to thicken and turns a light golden colour. Test by dipping the tip of a knife in the syrup. It is ready when removing the knife trails a candy floss like thread. Remove the pan from the heat and keep it warm. Whisk the egg whites in a food processor or mixer until they are semi-stiff. Turn down the speed of the machine and slowly pour the boiled syrup down the side of the bowl into the meringue. Turn up the machine speed a little and continue to whisk until the mixture is very stiff and forms peaks when the whisk is removed.

Remove the Alaska from the freezer. Load the meringue into a piping bag with a star nozzle and cover the Alaska with meringue, piping from the centre down to the edge. Return it to the freezer until required.

Preheat the oven to 200°C/gas mark 6. Put the remaining eau-de-vie de framboise into a saucepan. Bake the Alaska for 5-6 minutes until it is lightly coloured. Meanwhile, heat the eau-de-vie over a low flame. Take the Baked Alaska to the table. Carefully light the eau-de-vie with a match and pour it over the Baked Alaska, let the flames burn out and serve.

Bramley Apple Crumble
with Devonshire Clotted Cream

For the Sablé Pastry
185 g unsalted butter
225 g icing sugar
3 medium egg yolks
300 g plain flour

For the Apple Filling
50 g unsalted butter
6 large Bramleys, peeled, cored
   and roughly chopped
150 g caster sugar

For the Crumble Topping
80 g unsalted butter, finely diced
55 g ground almonds
110 g caster sugar
155 g plain flour

To Serve
300 g Devonshire clotted cream

First make the sablé pastry. In a food processor, mixer or by hand, cream the butter and icing sugar together until smooth. Add the egg yolks, mix well, then fold in the flour. Press the dough into a ball and refrigerate it for a couple of hours.

To assemble, grease a 25-cm tart tin or 8 individual ones. Roll the sablé pastry on a floured table to 5 mm thick. Line the tin(s) with the pastry, trim the edges and refrigerate for 2-3 hours.

Meanwhile, for the filling, melt the butter in a pan, put in the apples and cook them until they are soft. Remove them from the heat and stir in the sugar. Put all the crumble ingredients in a food processor or mixer and process until they look like breadcrumbs.

Pre-heat the oven to 175°C/gas mark 4. Line the cases with greaseproof paper, fill with baking beans and bake blind for 10-15 minutes until the pastry is light golden. Remove the beans and the paper and fill the cases with the warm apple mixture. Sprinkle over the crumble and bake for 20-30 minutes until the top is golden brown. Serve with the Devonshire clotted cream.

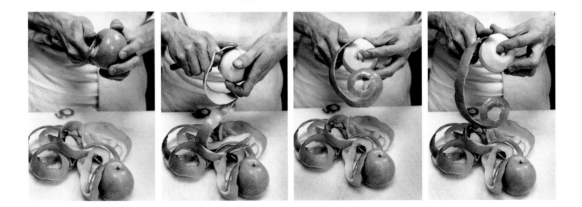

Preceding page: Baked Alaska

Cappuccino Brûlé

Not the easiest of desserts to make but once it is assembled it is simple to serve and can be made a day in advance.

For the Brûlé	For the Pastry Cream Brûlé Topping
5 medium egg yolks	150 ml milk
75 g caster sugar	30 g caster sugar
230 ml double cream	1 medium egg yolk
230 ml milk	10 g plain flour
15 g ground coffee	10 g cornflour
15 g instant coffee	250 ml double cream, semi-whipped
	8 tbsp demerara sugar
	$^1/_2$ split vanilla pod or 2 drops of vanilla essence

Pre-heat the oven to 150°C/gas mark 2.

Make the Brûlé first. Whisk together the egg yolks and sugar. Then in a saucepan mix the cream and milk with both the coffees, and bring it to the boil. Add this to the egg mixture and stir well. Pour it through a fine strainer to remove the coffee grounds, and then into eight large coffee or tea-cups to half-way up the sides.

Stand the cups in a bain-marie of hot water - a deep roasting tin would be good for this - and cover them with a sheet of foil. Bake for 40-50 minutes or until the Brûlés are firm. Remove the cups from the bain-marie and allow them to cool.

Now prepare the pastry cream. Bring the milk to the boil with the vanilla. Mix together the sugar and egg yolk then stir in the flour and cornflour. Pour the boiling milk on to the egg mixture and whisk together. Return the mixture to the pan over a low heat for 1 minute, stirring constantly until it thickens. Remove the vanilla pod if using. Pour it quickly into the blender and process until it is very smooth. Transfer the mixture into a bowl and cover it with a sheet of cling-film actually on the pastry cream to prevent it forming a skin. When it is cold, fold in the semi-whipped cream.

Spoon the pastry cream about 2 cm thick on to each of the Brûlés, using the back of the spoon to smooth it. Sprinkle a thin layer of brown sugar on each, then caramelise it with a blow torch or by placing it under a hot grill for a few minutes. Stand the cups on their saucers with a teaspoon and serve.

Caramelised Bread and Butter Pudding

575 ml double cream
575 ml full cream milk
pinch ground nutmeg
285 g caster sugar
6 medium eggs
110 g evaporated milk

1 French stick or baguette, thinly sliced and
   lightly spread with unsalted butter
145 g sultanas, soaked in water overnight
250 g light treacle or golden syrup

Preheat the oven to 150°C/gas mark 2. Bring the cream, milk and nutmeg to the boil and remove from the heat. Mix the sugar and eggs and whisk them into the warm cream mixture. Stir in the evaporated milk.

Lay slices of bread either in 8 strong teacups or in an ovenproof dish approximately 25 cm square and 6 cm deep. Scatter the sultanas over the top. Pour the cream mixture over the bread almost to the top of the dish and let it stand for a few minutes. Place the pudding(s) in a bain-marie of hot water – a deep roasting tray would be good – then into the oven.

Individual puddings will take 50–60 minutes to cook, and a large one approximately 80 minutes.

When the pudding(s) are set and golden brown, remove them from the oven and leave them to cool. Turn out individual ones on to plates or spoon a large one straight from the dish. Pour a little treacle or golden syrup over each portion and serve.

Rice Pudding with Armagnac Prunes

200 g pudding rice
100 g caster sugar
1 vanilla pod, split and seeds scraped out
pinch ground nutmeg
1.2 ltr milk

200 g stoned prunes,
   soaked in 600 ml water overnight
220 ml double cream
360 g evaporated milk
50 ml Armagnac
1 tsp arrowroot

Pre-heat the oven to 160°C/gas mark 3. Put the rice, 80 g of the caster sugar, the vanilla pod and its seeds, the nutmeg and milk into a pan, bring it to the boil and simmer for 20 minutes.

Meanwhile, simmer the prunes in their soaking water with 20 g of the caster sugar for 25 minutes. Add the cream and evaporated milk to the rice, bring it back to the boil and transfer the mixture to an oven dish. Cover it and bake for 40 minutes, stirring every so often. Pour the Armagnac over the prunes. Mix the arrowroot with a little water, stir it into the prune mixture and continue to simmer for another 10–15 minutes. If the liquid becomes too thick, add a little water. Serve the rice either hot or warm and spoon the prunes on top.

Cinnamon Roasted Fruits with Mascarpone

16 dried figs	1 cinnamon stick
32 dried apricots	10 g ground cinnamon
32 prunes, stoned	1 pineapple, peeled, cored and
50 g butter	cut into 2 cm cubes
200 g caster sugar	500 g mascarpone

Place all the dried fruit in water overnight to soften, then drain. Melt the butter in a pan, add the sugar and cook gently over a low heat, stirring occasionally, until the butter and sugar caramelise. Break the cinnamon stick into pieces, reserve a few bits for decoration and add the rest to the caramel with the ground cinnamon. Remove the pan from the heat and allow it to cool for 5 minutes. Add 75 ml warm water slowly to the caramel, followed by all the fruit, including the pineapple, and return the pan to the heat. Cook the fruits gently, giving an occasional stir, for about 10 minutes until well glazed.

Place the fruit on plates and garnish with the reserved cinnamon stick, a little of the caramel sauce and a spoonful of mascarpone.

Gooseberry and Elderflower Fool

For the Fool	For the Gooseberry Compote
150 ml white wine	300 g gooseberries
60 ml elderflower cordial	50 g caster sugar
juice of ¼ lemon	20 ml elderflower cordial
70 g caster sugar	
500 ml double cream	

To prepare the gooseberry compote, cook all the ingredients together slowly on a low heat, for 10 minutes until a jam-like consistency is achieved. Leave it to cool.

Mix together the white wine, elderflower cordial, lemon juice and sugar. Add the cream and whip the mixture slowly with an electric whisk. Then fold three-quarters of the compote into the cream mixture, pour it into glasses or a serving dish, and chill for 1-2 hours. Serve with the rest of the compote on top of the fool.

Scandinavian Iced Berries
with Hot White Chocolate Sauce

This was invented on the recommendation of a customer, who had had something similar in Sweden. The kitchen experimented for ages with the sauce until they came up with the melted white chocolate buttons. This is the simplest and most moreish pudding you will ever make and could become a dinner-party classic.

For this recipe you can buy either mixed frozen berries or raspberries. Alternatively, freeze your own selection of berries on a flat tray then put them into a bag in the freezer and use them on a rainy day. Larger berries, such as strawberries and big blackberries, are not recommended for this recipe as they do not defrost quickly enough.

1 kg frozen berries (100-120 g per person)	**For the Sauce** 600 g good quality white chocolate buttons 600 ml double cream

Place the chocolate buttons and the cream in a bowl over a pan of simmering water for 20-30 minutes, stirring every so often. When the sauce is hot, we are ready to go.

Five minutes before serving, put the berries on to dessert plates and leave at room temperature to lose a little of their chill. Transfer the chocolate sauce into a serving jug. Place the berries in front of your guests and pour the hot chocolate sauce at the table. Insist that you cover the berries generously for the best result.

Mousse aux Deux Chocolats

This recipe came back with Chris from a visit he made to New York in 1983. Most London restaurants offered a variation of chocolat au pot, or chocolate mousse, which has been superseded by more complicated puddings. This one has survived on merit.

150 g good quality white chocolate buttons	220 g caster sugar
80 g butter	4 g leaf gelatine
200 g good quality dark chocolate buttons	280 ml double cream, half whipped
8 medium eggs	4 Chocolate Flakes, broken up

In a bowl over a pan of simmering water melt the white chocolate and 50 g of the butter. Repeat the process with the dark chocolate and the remaining 30 g of butter. Whisk together the eggs and sugar until they are light and fluffy. Soak the gelatine in water for 1 minute, squeeze out, then melt in a bowl over hot water, and add it to the white chocolate mixture. Allow both of the chocolate mixtures to cool a little. Divide the egg mixture into two bowls. In one, fold in the dark chocolate mixture and half of the cream until it is well combined, cover and refrigerate until firm. In the other bowl, fold in the white chocolate mixture and the rest of the cream, cover and refrigerate until firm. To serve, take a large dessertspoon, dip it in warm water and take a spoonful of dark chocolate mousse. Put it on a plate and sprinkle some Flake over the top. Put a spoonful of the white chocolate mousse next to the dark one and sprinkle with Flake.

Amaretto Chocolate Truffles

A neat chocolate hit to finish with for those who don't want the full pudding. Most restaurants hand these out with the coffee whether you want them or not, but the Ivy decided that rather than hiding the cost of them in the bill, you should pay only for what you eat and not for what everyone else has. When you make the Amaretto Chocolate Truffles, use good-quality dark chocolate - as a general rule, the more expensive it is, the better the taste.

400 g good quality dark chocolate, finely chopped up	25 g unsalted butter, softened to room temperature
80 ml milk	40 ml Amaretto di Saronno
80 ml double cream	85g cocoa powder, mixed and sifted with 20 g icing sugar

Place 300 g of the chocolate into a clean bowl. Put the cream and milk together in a pan and bring it to the boil, then pour it on to the chocolate and stir until it is smooth and well emulsified. Stir in the butter and the Amaretto. Allow the mixture to cool to enable it to be piped.

Take a piping bag with a plain 1 cm nozzle, fill it with the chocolate mixture and pipe it in straight lines on to a tray, lined with greaseproof paper. Leave it in the fridge until firm enough to handle. Melt the remaining chocolate in a bowl over a pan of boiling water and allow to cool a little. Cut the set chocolate truffle mixture into 5-cm lengths, dip each piece into the melted chocolate then roll it in the cocoa powder. Ideally, this is done by hand, wearing disposable gloves. Alternatively, use a fork.

Tiramisu

A classic Italian pudding that Ivy regulars love. They protest when it is taken off the menu. Everyone does it in almost the same way - at least, they use the same ingredients but the results are different.

50 ml water	**For the Coffee Syrup**
215 g caster sugar	100 ml water
4 medium eggs, separated	100 g caster sugar
1.2 kg mascarpone cheese	10 g instant coffee
3 drops good-quality vanilla essence	20 g ground coffee
1 x 25 cm Vanilla Sponge Cake (see page 180)	50 ml Tia Maria
40 g cocoa powder	or similar coffee liqueur

First, place all the ingredients for the syrup in a saucepan with 100 ml water, bring it to the boil and simmer for 5 minutes. Turn off the heat and leave the syrup to infuse for 10 minutes. Strain it and put to one side.

Then bring the 50 ml water to the boil with 115 g of the caster sugar, stirring occasionally. Continue boiling until the syrup starts to thicken and turns a light golden colour. Test by dipping the tip of a knife in the syrup. It is ready when removing the knife trails a candyfloss-like thread. Remove the pan from the heat.

Meanwhile, in a food processor or mixer, whisk the egg yolks until they are fluffy. With the machine still running, slowly pour the boiled sugar syrup down the side of the bowl on to the egg yolks and continue to whisk until the mixture is light and fluffy again. Continue to whisk until the mixture has cooled to lukewarm. Slow the machine, put in the mascarpone and vanilla essence, and process until the mixture is smooth.

Remove the mixture from the machine. Wash and dry the bowl and the whisk attachment thoroughly.

Whisk the egg whites and the remaining caster sugar in the machine until they are fairly stiff, then slowly fold in the mascarpone mix.

Cut the sponge with a sharp bread knife horizontally into three $\frac{1}{2}$ cm-thick discs. Put one piece of sponge in the bottom of a serving dish – trim to fit. Soak the sponge with a third of the coffee syrup then spread on top a third of the mascarpone mixture. Repeat with the other two pieces of sponge. You can pipe on the last layer of mascarpone for a better visual effect.

Refrigerate the Tiramisu for 3–4 hours. Serve dusted with cocoa powder.

Sticky Toffee Pudding

The Black Forest Gâteau of the nineties. At least half a dozen restaurants claim to be the originators of this incredibly popular pudding. The Ivy isn't one of them. They do, however, make one of the best, layering the toffee with the sponge. In the restaurant the pudding is served individually. This is time-consuming and a bit fiddly, so it is recommended that you make a large pudding and cut it into individual servings.

For the Date Purée
375 g stoned dates
375 ml water

For the Toffee Sauce
640 ml double cream
340 g caster sugar
130 g liquid glucose (optional)
130 g unsalted butter

For the Sponge
130 g unsalted butter (removed from the fridge)
375 g soft dark brown sugar
3 medium eggs, lightly beaten
450 g strong plain flour   }
10 g baking powder   } sifted together
3 g bicarbonate of soda   }

First prepare the date purée. Simmer the dates in the water over a low heat for 10-15 minutes until they are soft and the water has almost evaporated. Process them in a blender until they are smooth.

Preheat the oven to 175°C/gas mark 4.

Now make the toffee sauce. Pour half the cream and the other ingredients into a thick-bottomed pan and mix well. Bring the sauce to the boil, stirring with a wooden spoon, and continue to boil until it is golden brown. Remove from the heat, allow it to cool slightly, then whisk in the remaining cream.

Grease and line a baking tin, measuring approximately 30 x 24 x 6cm deep, with greaseproof paper. Now make the sponge. In a food processor or mixer, cream the butter and sugar with the paddle on a medium speed until it is light and fluffy. Add the eggs slowly, taking care that the mixture does not separate. (If this does happen, add a little of the flour and continue mixing for a minute or so.) Then fold in the sifted flour mixture slowly until smooth. Finally, add the warm date purée and mix well.

Spread the mixture in the prepared tin and bake for about 50–60 minutes or until the sponge is firm to the touch. Allow to cool – it can be left in the tin. Remove the sponge from the tin and trim the outside edges. Cut it horizontally into three, then reassemble it in the baking tin, spreading two-thirds of the sauce between the layers.

Once you have assembled the pudding, reheat it in the oven at 175°C/gas mark 4 for 15-20 minutes, then cut it into eight equal servings and top with the remaining toffee sauce. Serve the Sticky Toffee Pudding with ice cream, soured cream or crème fraîche.

Savouries

Hardly any restaurants serve savouries any more. They are fossils from a time when dinner would regularly take four or five hours. Even though they are a minority taste now, customers still like to see them at the end of the menu, adding a sort of anchoring gravitas. Instead of having them after pudding, as is traditional, some people have them instead, particularly if they are in the middle of a good bottle of serious red wine, which would be humiliated by anything sweet.

Welsh Rarebit

150 g Cheddar cheese, grated	6 drops Tabasco
3 medium egg yolks	30 ml Guinness
1 tbsp Worcestershire sauce	8 slices bread – a small bloomer-style loaf is ideal
1 tsp English mustard	salt and pepper

Mix together all of the ingredients, except the bread, and season to taste. Toast the bread on both sides, spread the cheese mixture on top, about 1 cm thick, and grill until browned.

Reggiano Parmesan with Pickled Plum Tomatoes

When buying Parmesan or Parmigiano, go for Reggiano. This is the best – anything that does not call itself Reggiano is not true Parmesan. Pickle the tomatoes one week in advance.

12 plum tomatoes	5 g rosemary
or 24 pieces of sun-dried tomatoes	5 g thyme
100 ml balsamic vinegar	700-800 g Reggiano Parmesan
100 ml white wine vinegar	
50 g demerara sugar	

Pre-heat the oven to 110°C/gas mark ¼ or its lowest possible temperature. Halve the plum tomatoes, lay them on the grill rack and put them in the very cool oven. Leave them overnight so that they dry out. Bring to the boil the two vinegars, sugar, rosemary and thyme, then leave it to cool. Put the tomatoes in a dish and pour over the vinegar mixture. Leave for 1 week. If you are using sun-dried tomatoes, soak them in boiling water for 2 hours, then marinate as you would for plum tomatoes. Cut the Parmesan into rough chunks and serve either on a large dish or on individual plates with the tomatoes and some good crusty bread or rocket leaves.

Farmhouse Cheddar
with Crumpets and Onion Chutney

For the Crumpets
250 ml milk
15 g fresh yeast
250 ml water
450 g plain flour
pinch bicarbonate of soda
1 tsp salt

700-800 g good farmhouse Cheddar cheese
Onion Chutney (see recipe)

Onion Chutney
vegetable oil for frying
5 large red onions, peeled and finely chopped
1 clove garlic, peeled and crushed
50 g fresh root ginger, peeled and finely chopped
10 g thyme, leaves removed and chopped
$\frac{1}{2}$ tsp mustard seeds
pinch ground cloves
$\frac{1}{2}$ tsp ground cumin
75 ml sherry vinegar
75 ml balsamic vinegar
1 tbsp brown sugar
1 tbsp redcurrant jelly
1 tsp tomato purée
150 ml water
1 tsp cornflour

Warm a little of the milk and dissolve the yeast in it. Then add the rest of the milk and water. Put the flour into a food processor or mixer and slowly add the milk mixture. Process for a couple of minutes until it is smooth.

Add the bicarbonate of soda and the salt and mix it in. Pour the crumpet batter into a bowl and put it in a warm place for 30–40 minutes – the mix should be fermenting a little by now and covered in little bubbles.

Lightly oil a thick-bottomed frying-pan and some egg rings, and fill each ring to a third full. Cook the crumpets gently on both sides until they are light golden. Reheat them in the oven or under the grill before serving.

To serve, warm the crumpets in the oven or toast them under a hot grill. Serve them with a good chunk of Cheddar and a spoonful of the chutney. Alternatively, serve the Cheddar sliced on the crumpets with the chutney.

To make the Chutney: Heat some vegetable oil in a pan and gently cook the onions, garlic, ginger and all the herbs and spices until they are soft. Add the vinegars, the sugar, the redcurrant jelly, tomato purée and water. Simmer gently for 20 minutes. Mix the cornflour with a little water and stir it into the chutney. Continue to simmer for 40 minutes until the liquid has almost evaporated.

Remove the pan from the heat and cool the chutney. Serve within a few days or store in a Kilner jar in the fridge.

Herring Roes on Toast

Herring roes, or milts, are normally sold frozen or defrosted but occasionally can be found fresh during the spring and early summer months. The frozen ones cook quite nicely and, treated correctly, no one will know.

---

1 kg herring roes
350 g butter
salt and pepper
8 slices bread – a small bloomer-style loaf
220 g capers
20 g parsley, washed and finely chopped

Dry the herring roes on some kitchen paper. Heat 50 g of the butter in one large or two smaller frying pans (or cook the roes in batches).

Season the roes and cook them on a medium heat until they are golden brown (about 7 minutes) – they will curl up during cooking.

Meanwhile toast the bread on both sides. When the roes are ready pile them on the toast. Melt the rest of the butter in the pan, add the capers and parsley, and spoon it over the roes.

Scotch Woodcock

I have a long-standing disagreement about the construction of Scotch Woodcock. I think the anchovy should be mashed, as in Gentlemen's Relish, and only the yolks of the eggs used. I'd also use capers, not olives. However, this is *The Ivy Cookbook*, so here is their recipe.

---

8 medium eggs
60 ml double cream
90 g butter
salt and pepper

8 slices bread - a small bloomer-style loaf is
  ideal
16 anchovy fillets, cut in half lengthways
12 stoned green olives, sliced

Crack the eggs into a bowl and whisk them. Stir in the cream and season the mixture.

In a thick-bottomed pan, melt 60 g of the butter, add the egg mixture and stir over a medium heat with a wooden spoon, ensuring that you scrape the sides occasionally. The eggs should be creamy when they are cooked.

Meanwhile, toast the bread on both sides and butter it. Spoon the eggs on to the toast and arrange the anchovies in a lattice on top. Lay the olives over the anchovies and serve.

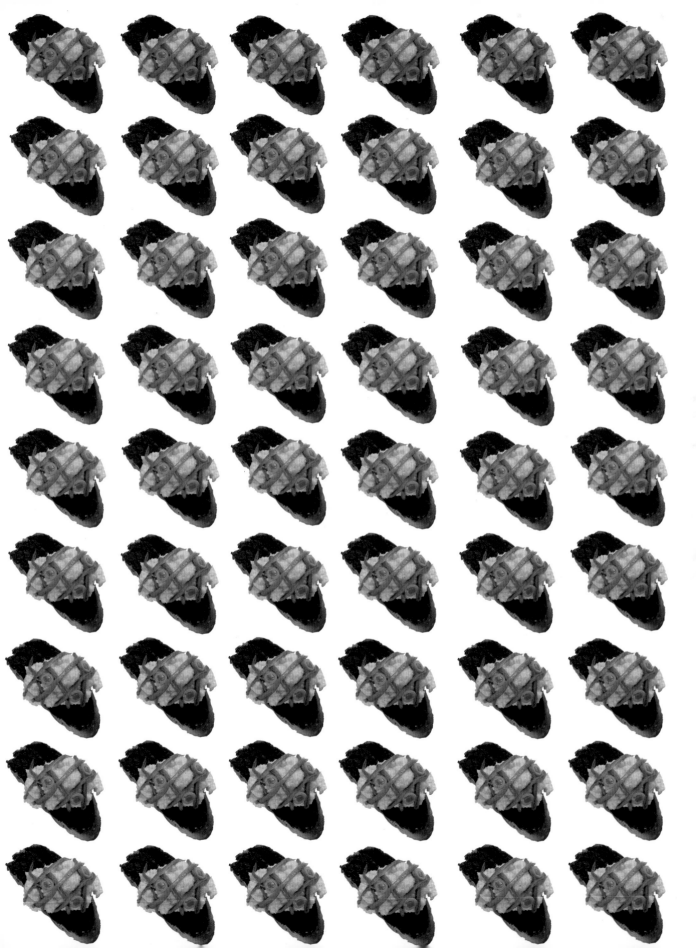

10.30 P.M. Tables are turning. The non-theatre diners are departing and the theatre crowd arrives. The bar is a seethe of acquaintances passing.

> 'How was it?'
> 'How was the duck?'
> 'How was the leading lady?'

The atmosphere changes, the temperature rises a notch. It is the end of a special evening for most of these customers. Theatre programmes lie ostentatiously on the corners of tables.

11.00 P.M. The first-night party arrives with a bantering clamour like a lot of RADA students making their first entrance as Montagues and Capulets. An opening night at a small, trendy, sold-out theatre. The star, a young man tipped for Hollywood, is surrounded by attendant males and a droopy girl with bad skin and dead eyes. The director is all arms, like a man herding pigs. They settle at the table and immediately get up again to say hello to friends. The room is suddenly a junior school of waving hands and eyes searching for a meet. The peripheral tables look on and beam like proud parents at a sports day. This is what they come to the Ivy for. The young actor looks up and – through his famously long lashes, freshly glued with cold cream – sees his glittering future unfold in a string of adoring Ivy dinners. Chris raises his eyebrows to the waiter. Champagne. On the house.

11.45 P.M. Just two tables to go. The manager thinks one may be a no-show, the other has called to say they'll be late. They're reminded that the kitchen closes at twelve. They want to order from the car.

> The kitchen's pretty firm about not taking orders after twelve.
> 'We stop at twelve, not ten past.'
> An order at midnight could mean pudding going on till one thirty.

Downstairs, it's beginning to slow down enough for the chefs to think about home and night buses. The porters, though, are at full stretch. The big blue crates of detritus stack up. Everything that isn't eaten gets shovelled into these trays. A thick gloop of pudding and stew and bones, plates and cutlery. The plongeur hefts them to the sink and hoses them down with the industrial shower, trying to pick out the bits that aren't supposed to go down the waste disposal. Those blasted soy-sauce dishes. Another porter humps bags of rubbish out of the service entrance into the street for the late-night bin men. There is a notice warning them not to put too many bones in the bags. If you ever find yourself needing to get rid of an awkward body, leave it in a bin bag outside the Ivy. No one would notice.

12.30 A.M. Upstairs in the function room the private party breaks up, drunkenly. A record producer with a grey ponytail and Chardonnay down his Comme des Garçons shirt takes a waiter aside and makes him promise faithfully to pass on his compliments to the chef.

> 'That spag we gave you the recipe for was brilliant, brilliant. He made it very well, really. Almost as good as in New York. You should put it on the menu and name it after the star. Good little diary item, that.
> 'Get your PR to call my PR.'

The flashguns briefly light up the street outside. The doorman stands back.

1.00 A.M. The restaurant's nearly empty now. Half a dozen tables linger over coffee. One of the girls with big bosoms has joined a table with two journalists. Her friends left an hour ago to go clubbing. The man she's interested in is a gossip columnist. He's telling her thirteen things they couldn't print about the young first-night star. His colleague yawns and thinks about slipping away. The girl sits with her chin on her hand and her chest resting on the hack's arm. She isn't listening.

1.30 A.M. The waiters wait until the last customer has left before beginning to tuck up the room for the night. No late diner is ever asked to leave, will ever have to sit amongst stacking chairs or even see a waiter yawn a reproach, but finally the last couple slowly make their way to the door and their cab; the hat check smiles, hands them their coats and the door clicks shut. Their coffee cups are cleared away and the lights come up. The brightness is strange - you expect the room to fade slowly to black - but when the house lights come on the spirit of the drama is still palpable. The table cloths come off and suddenly the air conditioning cuts out. All day it has been a blank white hiss, almost unnoticeable beneath the eddying noise of the restaurant. Now the silence lets in the arbitrary ambient sounds of the early morning city – the clank and howl of traffic, a drunk singing 'Guide me, O Thou Great Redeemer' somewhere down by a lap-dancing bar, the beep beep of a reversing rubbish truck. The sounds of London filter in like drizzle rinsing away the ghosts of dinner. Being in an empty restaurant after service makes you wonder how the noise and laughter can go so utterly fast, their absence almost as noticeable as their presence. Little things jump into focus – a curl of cigar ash under a table, a cork left on a window-sill, the dimpled imprint of a back on a sofa, the archaeology of conviviality and hospitality. A dining room emptied of dinner and diners slumps into a sort of reverie and perhaps reminds you of the long chain of events, ambitions, achievements, toils and luck that must come together to make a public meal, not just in the immediate sense of this food and these people, but in the wider sense that society has grown to see food and company as socially synonymous. Eating is the only essential bodily function that we seek to do in the company of strangers, with its ancient lines of unwritten but communally understood rituals and manners that have to be implicitly agreed for a restaurant to function.

1.45 A.M. Downstairs in the staff dining room four waiters and a couple of cooks slouch over their on-the-house cans of beer and chain-lit fags. The exhaustion is palpable. They sit in their street clothes, unwilling to depart finally into the cold, quiet night. They talk in disjointed sentences, the runner going through the tipped tray for the umpteenth time.

> 'By this much, this much; it's the cassoulet plates.'
> Slowly, in ones and twos, they make their way.
> 'Are you off tomorrow?'
> 'No, early.'
> 'Oh, bad luck.'

In the kitchen only the porters are left swabbing the floors. Stripped to the waist, with their little white hats, they look like American sailors. The laundry is piled into bags, the fridges and store cupboards locked. The white neon hums.

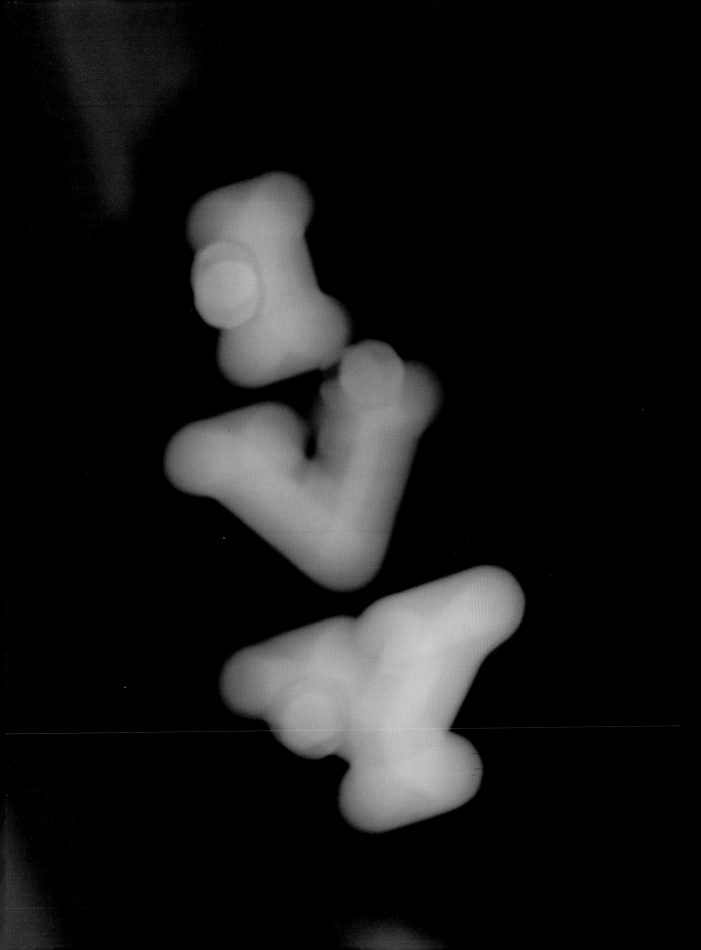

2.00 A.M. In the restaurant only the manageress and one of the waiters are left. Beautiful as a Manet, she sits with her head on one side, filling in the log.

'A good evening. Atmosphere fun. Sir Rowland was in looking well. First night of Past Tense. Comped champagne. Runner dropped tray behind Table Fifteen, just missed them – no casualties. Kitchen coped well. Ran out of serving spoons. Everyone turned up.'

She puts the book away and goes down to hurry the porters. The waiter sits on the bar and kicks his heels. Behind him the ashtrays and coffee cups drip dry.

2.30 A.M. The manageress, with her collection of keys, checks everything for the last time, switches off the lights in the restaurant and punches the alarm box. She opens the back door. Cold air rushes in and the alarm whines.

In the last eighteen hours, the kitchen and the restaurant have prepared, served and cleared away eighty kilos of potatoes; a hundred kilos of beef and veal bones; ten kilos of fish-cake mix; ten kilos of sugar; thirty heads of lettuce; thirteen kilos of flour; fifty Caesar Salads; twenty-one Bang-Bang Chickens; ten Potted Shrimps; one portion of caviar; twenty-four Liver and Bacon; eight Hamburgers; ten Kedgerees; a dozen Poulets; eighty portions of chips; four hundred cups of coffee; ninety glasses of champagne; ten cases of water. They have got through twenty loo rolls; ten light-bulbs; eighty-two Singapore orchids; a hundred and fifteen pounds' worth of electricity and two hundred pounds' worth of clean linen; twenty-nine bin bags; ten litres of washing-up liquid; one kilo of chocolate truffles.

Eighty-two staff have fed four hundred and twenty-five people, using up six months' worth of man-hours. They've written 'Happy Birthday' in chocolate on three plates and used four blue plasters. Eight glasses and four plates have been broken, but no one died. One person has been fired, one left. No one's had a baby. There were three marriage proposals: one yes, one no, one don't know.

The manageress turns the key in the lock. For a moment the street is silent, and then, muffled in the distance, they hear the telephone ring. Nobody has ever had the time or the inclination to count how many telephone calls there are in a day. The manageress and the waiter walk down the empty street. As they reach the corner, he snakes an arm round her waist. She looks up, they kiss.

Stage Door Johnny, Barry Flanagan (1990)

Index

Figures in italics refer to illustrations.